GREAT DIVIDES

Understanding the Controversies That Come Between Christians

RONALD H. NASH

D1488998

NAVPRESS

BRINGING TRUTH TO LIFE
NavPress Publishing Group
P.O. Box 35001, Colorado Springs, Colorado 80935

The Navigators is an international Christian organization. Jesus Christ gave His followers the Great Commission to go and make disciples (Matthew 28:19). The aim of The Navigators is to help fulfill that commission by multiplying laborers for Christ in every nation.

NavPress is the publishing ministry of The Navigators. NavPress publications are tools to help Christians grow. Although publications alone cannot make disciples or change lives, they can help believers learn biblical discipleship, and apply what they learn to their lives and ministries.

© 1993 by Ronald H. Nash
All rights reserved. No part of this publication may be reproduced in any form without written permission from NavPress, P.O. Box 35001, Colorado Springs, CO 80935.
Library of Congress Catalog Card Number: 92-40957
ISBN 08910-96965

Cover illustration: Steven Eames

The text of chapter 5, "The Controversy Over Psychology and Counseling," was written by Steve Webb, © 1992 Steve Webb. Used by permission.

Unless otherwise identified, all Scripture in this publication is from the *Holy Bible: New International Version* (NIV). Copyright © 1973, 1978, 1984, International Bible Society. Used by permission of Zondervan Bible Publishers. Other versions used include: the *New American Standard Bible* (NASB), © The Lockman Foundation 1960, 1962, 1963, 1968, 1971, 1972, 1973, 1975, 1977; and the *King James Version* (KJV).

Nash, Ronald H.
   Great divides : understanding the controversies that come between Christians / Ronald H. Nash.
      p.   cm.
   Includes bibliographical references.
   ISBN 0-89109-696-5 :
   1. Evangelicalism. 2. Theology, Doctrinal. 3. Church controversies. 4. Christian union.   I. Title.
BR1640.N29   1993
273'.9—dc20   92-40957
                                                                CIP

Printed in the United States of America

CONTENTS

Introduction   7

1 The Controversy Over the Pro-Life Movement   17

2 The Controversy Over Women Leaders in the Church   39

3 The Controversy Over Radical Feminism   61

4 The Controversy Over Divorce and Remarriage   77

5 The Controversy Over Psychology and Counseling   93

6 The Controversy Over the Health and Wealth Gospel   109

7 The Controversy Over Christian Involvement
in Politics   127

8 The Controversy Over Christian Reconstructionists:
Are They Dangerous?   153

9 The Controversy Over Lordship Salvation   177

10 The Controversy Over the End Times:
What Does the Bible Really Say?   197

Epilogue   219

Notes   223

To
The Perry Children:
Donald, Betty Jane, JoAnn, JoNette, Linda,
and to the memory of Joyce

ACKNOWLEDGMENTS

Over a period of time spanning forty years, many people have helped shape the ideas that appear in this book. Near the beginning, there were the Godleys of Parma, Ohio. A bit later came Chick Kiloski who first introduced me to the convictions of one of my chapters; he knows which one. Then there were professors like Carlton Gregory and T. B. Crum who came along at a time when I began to think about the possibility of an academic career. There were the people in the churches I pastored and the ten thousand or so students I've taught over the years. There were Carl Henry and Gordon Clark. It was a privilege to know and learn from two of the truly great evangelical minds of the twentieth century. And there were all the other people who will read this and know I'm thinking of them as I write this page. And there was Steve Webb, the editor for so many of my earlier books, who saw the potential in the rough idea I had and who helped nurse that idea into this finished product. During an especially busy time when I was traveling and speaking in the former Soviet Union, Steve went beyond the call of duty and contributed the chapter on counseling in this book. And through it all, there was my family to help keep me on track: my wife, Betty Jane, our daughter, Jennifer, our son, Jeff, and our daughter-in-law, Cindy. Special thanks to all.

INTRODUCTION

---❖---

Sally found herself in a relational pickle. She had been eagerly building a friendship with her new neighbor, Jill. Things seemed headed in a positive direction, and Sally was especially pleased that her children got along well with Jill's. Just when Sally thought she had found a best friend in her neighborhood, she discovered Jill's views on some important issues were much different from her own.

Sally had considered herself a Christian since the time when she was involved with a campus ministry at the university. Now a single mother with two children, she worked hard to provide a good home for her son and daughter. She had just moved from the inner city to the suburbs of a large southwestern city. She had found what she perceived to be a warm and caring church, where she and the kids could find fellowship and comfort. She had spent the past two years working through the emotional devastation of a divorce and trying to improve her job situation. Now she found herself in a relationship that had quickly deteriorated from pleasant to at best uncomfortable.

Jill attended the same church Sally had found so warm.

Her strong views about Sally's situation had come out in a recent conversation, sending Sally into an emotional tailspin. "How can Jill think I was wrong to divorce Jim?" Sally was saying to herself one morning. "He was abusive to me and the kids; his drinking was out of control; and his continual affairs had humiliated our entire family. Why would anyone tell me I was wrong to divorce him? It was an intolerable situation. Even the Bible says so!"

Jill's view, of course, was based on her conviction that God hates divorce and that if reconciliation was at all possible, divorce was never right. This came out one day when Sally had told Jill that Jim was still calling, in spite of the court's restraining order, wanting to "come home." "You should let him," Jill had interjected. "Never!" Sally replied. Things had not been the same since. Now it seemed like the friendship that had developed between them in the last five months might be down the drain.

TEN CONTROVERSIES THAT DIVIDE CHRISTIANS

This book deals with ten controversies that come between Christians. These are *great divides* that can hurt relationships and cause people, like Sally and Jill, emotional turmoil and even lost fellowship. I have chosen ten of the most hotly debated topics among persons who consider themselves part of the church or the body of Christ. I doubt we could find anyone who considers himself or herself an informed Christian who would not be familiar with at least one or more of these controversies . . . and have a personal opinion. We'll look at these *great divides* in the following order:

1. The controversy over the pro-life movement
2. The controversy over the place of women in the church
3. The controversy over radical feminism

4. The controversy over divorce and remarriage
5. The controversy over psychology and counseling
6. The controversy over the health and wealth gospel
7. The controversy over Christian involvement
   in politics
8. The controversy over reconstructionism
9. The controversy over lordship salvation
10. The controversy over the end times

These issues are important because each involves questions that affect how we understand the Bible, touches our relationships with other Christians, and eventually influences how we live (our conduct both inside and outside the church).

Many believers find some of these controversies confusing. Others find themselves alienated, either emotionally or socially, from other believers over these issues. Some feel even stronger about them, to the degree that they may even refuse to have fellowship or worship with those who take positions on these issues that they consider "heretical" or "unbiblical."

Why do you believe what you do about abortion, perhaps the hottest issue of our day? Have you studied the issue in depth and come to a position that you think is consistent with your deeper beliefs? Do you believe that abortion is an act that generally does not "fit" with a scriptural ethic (perhaps you allow exceptions if a mother's life is in danger, or in cases like incest)? What are your views about divorce? As in the case of Jill and Sally above, would you tell an abused wife to go back to her husband, even though the consequences for her and her children might be dangerous?

Examining Your Deepest Beliefs
Have you carefully examined your deepest beliefs? What do you believe about the existence of God, about human nature, about how we know things, and about the course and nature of history? These deep beliefs help us form a consistent world-

view—one that is philosophically satisfying and practically beneficial. The closer our perceptions come to reality, the philosopher reasons, the better we'll be able to live, for we'll be in better harmony with our real environment. Reality for the Christian, of course, is usually seen through some sort of biblical lens, what many Christian teachers call a biblically informed world and life view.[1]

Perhaps you've been reading our society's more influential news sources, maybe a magazine like *Time* or *U.S. News & World Report*, or a newspaper like *The Wall Street Journal*. Those news sources often unintentionally provide support for the claim that our society has drifted from its moorings. That's why a book like this one is so important: it gets us thinking again, reflecting on those moorings. Its purpose is to help us grasp why we believe and think the way we do on ten of the most important and yet potentially divisive issues of our day. Perhaps it will help us reset our moorings, if need be, or deepen our convictions where appropriate. There are social benefits, too.

Christian thinker and pollster George Barna has done a number of significant studies on the current attitudes, thinking, trends, and values of the church today. None is more perceptive than his *The Frog in the Kettle*. Here is one of Barna's more trenchant insights:

> The '90s represent an ideal time for us to reinforce the basic aspects of our faith, emphasizing the application of such knowledge to a new mode of behavior and thought that reflects Jesus.
>
> One step in this direction would be to recast the prevailing perspective about our faith. During the '90s, positioning Christianity as a "religion" may do us more harm than good. This approach simply encourages people to categorize the elements of our faith as one among several "religious" options, and thereby limit

the influence of Christian principles and teachings
to the religious sphere of life. This enables people to
isolate the truths and demands of the faith from the
reality of every other dimension of their existence.
Christianity can be neatly boxed and laid aside, as
long as it is nothing more than a series of proverbs and
teachings about man, God, life, eternity and the like.[2]

I think Barna puts his finger on a couple of points here
that need to be amplified. One is that, indeed, Christianity—be
it in the 1990s or the 2020s—should never be "positioned" as
a religion, and certainly not by its adherents. The media will
do that for us. But his point is well taken: Christian faith is
essentially relationship with Jesus Christ and others in the body
of Christ.[3]

Barna also offers the cogent insight that if we were to position our Christian faith as just another religion, it would then be
but one more option among many: the new Hinduism, Buddhism,
Islam, the cults, etc. It is so important for us to remember that,
whether we're in the U.S. or on a mission trip to recently liberated
Russia or Eastern European countries, those in the world who
view us as Christ's ambassadors are looking for something different, something stable, something with solid moorings.

Barna goes on in his analysis:

If, however, we expand people's concept of Christianity so they view it as a life-style [or world view] and a
purpose, rather than as a theology, perhaps we would
challenge them to take our faith more seriously. To
a great extent, we will be taken only as seriously as
we expect people to take us. If we can help the world
to recognize that our faith is not a one dimensional
experience, but is a multi-faceted way of life which
permeates every thought, action and experience,
Christianity would not only assume greater importance

in the minds of people, but would challenge non-believers to explore this faith in a new way.[4]

I agree in large part, but I must admit, this idea of looking beyond the theology of the Christian faith takes a while to settle in a crusty old theologian and philosopher like myself. Yet, clearly, as I reflect on my own life, my prayers, my study, the Christian faith has always entailed a certain lifestyle, a multifaceted way of life that permeates my thoughts, actions, and experience. Of course, Christianity is much more than this. It also entails an objective reality outside of myself that includes the reality of God's existence and the truth revealed to us in His Word.

It is, I hope, your desire as well to see Christ in every aspect of your life. Our faith is not simply the study of God and His ways but the application of His ways to our lives, learning to think great thoughts about God, and learning to get along with His people, as varied and different as they are.

Dealing with the Great Divides
I've written this book to help you think through some of the toughest issues we face today as a church. As we move through the ten issues I've picked out (I could have added five more), my hope is that you'll allow your mind to be open to other views. The issues themselves can be divisive. I also hope you'll realize something about God in each of these chapters: about His character and His sovereignty. What do you believe He thinks about these issues?

What About Christian Unity?
As a church, we Christians should seek to demonstrate unity to the outside world so that we make Christ attractive to the world, drawing others to Him through our love and unity. But love often means we must draw conclusions about some matters where Christians disagree. At the same time we should recog-

nize that many of these issues have the potential to divide us theologically. Some beliefs we'll encounter come dangerously close to what the Bible calls false teaching.

As we unpack these controversies, one of my goals is to show that these ten issues have the potential to undermine the unity of the body of Christ. Hence, they could also undermine our effectiveness as God's ambassadors to the world. But some of these issues should never be divisive, since those on each side of the disagreement could be considered orthodox. For example, I may disagree heartily with someone on the issue of the end times, but to allow that issue to divide us in a way that breaks fellowship would be unjustifiable. But what if the person disagreeing with me took the position that Jesus was not God or would never return a second time to earth because He was incapable of doing so? My response to such an unbiblical position must be totally different.

We'll also touch on really hot issues, such as the health and wealth gospel, where many Bible-believing Christians will feel compelled to disagree.

We're discussing the difference between mountains and molehills. If a person disputes something as essential to orthodox Christian faith as, say, the deity of Christ or His bodily resurrection, then his view clearly contradicts Christian faith. In such a case, the person who holds such a position has clearly moved into what the apostle Paul called false teaching. Such teaching is to be avoided by all believers. I may choose to continue to try to persuade the person to move o a more orthodox viewpoint. But disagreements over such issues as the pretribulational rapture or a premillenial view of Jesus' return should not disrupt our fellowship in Christ.

CULTURAL DIVIDES

One important element that often influences the controversies raised in this book is cultural conditioning. The decisions we make about which side of the lordship salvation controversy we hold to, for example, may be conditioned by the cultural upbringing we've had. If our church taught a certain view, and we trust the pastor who did the teaching, then we may hold his view. On the other hand, if we hold to a certain view of science, it will decidedly affect how we think about the controversy over psychology and counseling. Or, if we believe that Christians should have nothing whatsoever to do with cultural issues, it will clearly affect how we view the controversy over Christian involvement in politics.

It is precisely at this point, on the issue of conditioning, that many believers stop personal analysis. There seems to be a refusal on our part to think that anything may have affected our thinking other than "the Bible and the Bible alone." Yet we walk around with world and life views that have been touched at many points by many things other than Scripture.

In some cases these pieces of cultural baggage have a benign effect—such as the fact that most of us use automobiles as transportation, even though cars aren't mentioned in the Bible. But at other points someone may decide, because of an eccentric *cultural* "principle" to avoid fellowship with someone else because that person crosses his or her theological "t's" at a slightly different angle. Others, like Sally in our opening story, pull away from certain positions (and people) because of the pain of facing cultural—or physical and emotional—realities.

We all need to dig deeper about how our cultural viewpoint, our personality bents, and our philosophical world and life view affect our thinking about the issues we're concerned with in this book. If we're to seek unity, to seek to be Christ's ambassadors, and to seek a hearing with skeptical unbelievers, we must at the very least seek to understand how other Christians view these important issues. That will go a long way toward lowering the barriers between unbelievers and the Christian faith. It may also demonstrate, at the very least, that we believers understand one another and are attempting to fulfill Christ's Great Commandment, that we love one another.

THE LAYOUT OF THIS WORK

I hope you've gathered from this discussion that I'm concerned about unity in the body of Christ despite our diversity on certain issues. I now wish to emphasize one statement regarding love: There are times when love obliges us to honestly confront one another with our disagreements. Generally, throughout this book, I will not be shy about stating my own position with regard to an issue. Likewise, I will at times take issue with other believers on areas where we disagree. I do that in order to advance the important dialogue on these critical issues facing the church today. In most cases, I do not state my own position or question that of others in order to raise doubts about another Christian's spirituality or leadership. What I do has the purpose of encouraging dialogue and, as the Proverbs say, "sharpening one another." With my editor's help I have sought to phrase these criticisms in a sensitive way that clarifies the differences between honorable people. Naturally, I accept responsibility for any oversights of this approach.

Finally, I should warn you that, when necessary, I do not shy away from warning the church about what I believe are heretical or false teachings that could damage the body. This is, of course, an expression of what I understand as my responsibility as a Christian teacher. Given the diversity of people who will read this book, some disagreement with my views is understandable. If you disagree with my viewpoint but gain some insight into how and why others think about these issues, I will have accomplished one objective of this book. If you go on from there and are able to affirm the dignity of others who do disagree with you (or me), then perhaps even greater things will be accomplished.

Chapter One

THE CONTROVERSY OVER THE PRO-LIFE MOVEMENT

❖

R ecent television news clips show pro-life supporters being roughed up and dragged away from the front sidewalks of abortion clinics in places like Wichita, Kansas, Milwaukee, Wisconsin, and Buffalo, New York. These pro-life protesters are not being manhandled by the police, but by pro-choice advocates! Is there something in the pro-life position that makes its followers deserve this sort of treatment?

Certainly, the first thing these reports should do is to cause us to consider the gravity of taking a pro-life position. Second, the vehemence over this issue on both sides, and the current controversy that rages over whether the *Roe v. Wade* decision legalizing abortion will remain in force, makes the abortion issue the largest of the great divides. Many Christians fail to realize, however, that some people who make claim to the Christian faith are clearly not on the pro-life side. In fact, some who consider themselves evangelical Christians reject the pro-life position in favor of the pro-choice side. We're not talking about the fuzzy areas here—those issues of whether to allow abortion in the cases of incest or when the mother's life is in danger. We're speaking of evangelicals who claim that abortion-on-demand is okay, even if only for convenience as a form of birth control!

Let's take a brief look at two very controversial aspects of this issue.

TWO SURPRISING POSITIONS
FROM EVANGELICALS

With the exception of some evangelical feminists and a few professors at evangelical colleges and seminaries, the majority of Christians seem to agree that abortion is a major social evil about which they cannot be silent. While some believe there is room for disagreement over what should be done in cases of rape or incest, almost all evangelical Christians agree that killing an unborn baby as a form of birth control, gender selection, or simply because it is unwanted is immoral. The major exception to this last claim are some extreme feminist evangelicals[1] who take the same sort of pro-abortion approach to the issue that a radical feminist might take. Some even support abortion-on-demand and abortion as a method of birth control.

A second, more subtle position is held by some evangelicals who call themselves "consistently pro-life."[2] The persons claiming this view oppose abortion. However, their consistently pro-life stance does not stop with abortion. Their extensive agenda includes opposition to nuclear weapons, economic injustice, environmental pollution, and substance abuse. Later in this chapter, we'll see the effect that this additional philosophical baggage has on the pro-life movement.

THE PRO-LIFE APPROACH
OF THE EVANGELICAL MAJORITY

According to a press release issued by the Barna Research Group just before the 1992 election, "Three quarters of all evangelicals (77%) strongly consider abortion to be morally wrong; a figure which is much higher than the 41% among non-evangelicals."

Elsewhere, Barna has written, "It is true that Christians are considerably more likely to be pro-life than pro-choice, but a significant minority of Christians support the position that the decision of whether to have an abortion is the woman's." In that same report, Barna pointed out that 50 percent of all Christians *disagreed* with the statement: "It is a woman's right to have an abortion." Only 19 percent of all Christians agreed with this statement strongly, but another 19 percent agreed somewhat. Twelve percent were undecided.[3]

The basic question I want to explore is why so many Protestant and Catholic Christians view abortion as an evil way to treat a fetus. What is it about this issue that ignites so much passion? And, why is it so critical that we seek unity on the issue?

The late Francis Schaeffer captured the spirit of millions of Christians when he and coauthor C. Everett Koop began their book *Whatever Happened to the Human Race?* with these words: "Cultures can be judged in many ways, but eventually every nation in every age must be judged by this test: how did it treat people? Each generation, each wave of humanity, evaluates its predecessors on this basis. The final measure of mankind's humanity is how humanely people treat one another."[4] According to Schaeffer,

What we regard as thinkable and unthinkable about how we treat human life has changed drastically in the West. For centuries Western culture has regarded human life and the quality of the life of the individual as special. It has been common to speak of "the sanctity of human life." Until recently in our own century, with some notable and sorry exceptions, human beings have generally been regarded as special, unique, and nonexpendable. But in one short generation we have moved from a generally high view of life to a very low one.[5]

The shift in values that Schaeffer laments is a reflection of the fact that American society has abandoned its Judeo-Christian base for a humanistic one that elevates humans and their wishes above God and His will. Americans now find themselves part of a culture that terminates more than one-and-a-half million fetuses a year. By the end of 1991, approximately twenty-eight million abortions had been performed in the United States since the *Roe v. Wade* decision in 1973. This statistic makes the Nazi Holocaust look like the work of rank amateurs.

If one believes that a fetus is a human being, one does not have to be a Christian to feel outrage at the carnage in the U.S. and to feel shame over what it reveals about the moral landscape of our nation. As Charles Colson stated, "When it comes to human life, Christians can't concede any ground. We are called to take up the cause of the weak, the helpless, the defenseless. It is our duty; that which, in large part, defines us as citizens of the kingdom of God. Christians, in short, must be unequivocally, resolutely, and unapologetically prolife."[6]

This is an issue where the vast majority of Catholic and Protestant Christians agree. Here is the primary support for the pro-life position that we are concerned about in this chapter:

1. The fetus is alive.
2. The fetus has a soul.
3. The Bible ascribes life and worth to the fetus (Psalm 139; Isaiah 49:1,5; Jeremiah 1:4-5).
4. Modern medicine has raised the status of the fetus, through neonatal technology, ultrasound, and even fetal surgery and fetal therapy, which take place within the womb.[7]
5. Even the legal system in the United States has

acknowledged the rights of the fetus through recognition of the impact on the fetus of the workplace, of alcohol or drug abuse by the mother, and of passive smoking. One woman was even convicted of "providing cocaine to another" because of the effects of her addiction on her unborn baby.[8]

6. Therefore, the fetus is an unborn, living person, deserving of our highest respect and care; and abortion is wrong.

7. In cases where extenuating circumstances exist (rape, incest, danger to the mother's life), great care should still be taken to protect the life of the fetus.

The following chart summarizes the various positions we see on this issue:

Total Reproductive Freedom	Abortion-on-Demand Allowed	Balanced Rights	Right-to-Life	Absolute Right-to-Life

To explain briefly, the "total reproductive freedom" stance says that the decision to abort has nothing to do with the status of the fetus; it is the woman's body and she is in full control; it is strictly her decision. Those who support the "abortion-on-demand" stance believe abortion should be allowed whenever the pregnant woman wishes. The "balanced rights" stance recognizes the gravity of the abortion decision and states that the woman's rights and child's rights must be weighed against one another; ultimately, of course, the decision is the woman's.

The "right-to-life" position allows abortion when a woman's life is endangered or the circumstances of conception might create serious psychological difficulties for both woman and child (rape, incest); but it asks the serious question whether the birth of a child (for the sake of both) or a future adoption (for the sake of the fetus) could redeem some good from a bad situation. This position seeks to prevent abortion in all but the most difficult circumstances.

The "absolute right-to-life" position says that abortion is never acceptable. The fetus is a person and an innocent victim whose life should always be protected. To abort an unborn baby is tantamount to murder.

THE AUTHOR'S VIEW

I've been saying that the vast majority of Christians line up somewhere on the right side of this chart, and that less than 15 percent of evangelicals would be to the left of the center of the chart (where balanced rights are demanded between the woman and the fetus). This illustrates the serious nature of the debate and the critical decision every Christian faces when weighing the issues involved. I think the biblical evidence and the weight of modern medical technology leave little room for those who consider themselves Christians to take any less than a right-to-life position. I agree with Colson: We must be unwaveringly pro-life.

I believe that because of the importance of unwavering Christian support on behalf of the unborn, evangelicals need to be alert to any attempt to weaken that support within their circles of influence. Therefore, it is very important to examine in more depth the two surprising positions a minority of evangelicals are taking on this issue. We will start with the views of the radical feminists.

GENDER-FEMINISTS AND THE ABORTION ISSUE

The position that almost all radical feminists take with regard to the unborn is a logical consequence of certain tenets of "gender-feminism," a cause we will examine in depth in chapter 3. The radical feminist view of abortion is particularly affected by their interpretation of the oppression they believe afflicts women. According to author Carol McMillan, "Radical feminists emphasize that the mere fact—that is, the biological fact—of being a woman is an oppressive one. The tyrant is not man at all but nature; men simply take advantage of the situation which is already weighted in their favour."[9] Support for McMillan's claim comes from feminist writer Shulamith Firestone: "The heart of woman's oppression is her child-bearing and child-rearing role."[10]

We must understand, in the overall scheme of things, what the radical feminists are really after. Statements like those of Firestone indicate that the only authentic way a woman can secure liberation from oppression requires that she first be liberated from being a woman! And so, as James L. Sauer explained, "Having rejected the nature of woman as she was divinely created, the feminist must, like Dr. Frankenstein, construct a new woman from her own imagination." This requires her to deny "that biology is destiny, because she denies that biology is designed. Feminism, in this sense, is akin to the humanistic assumptions found in the Communist vision of a new socialist man. Humanism of all types rebels against the notions of a created order, of biological roles, and of social limitation."[11]

What becomes clear, then, is that no argument of any kind in support of protecting the life of the fetus can possibly carry any weight for those who have surrendered to the ideology of gender-feminism. This fact helps to explain what many evangelicals find difficult to understand—namely, the stubbornly pro-abortion stance of large numbers of evangelical feminists.

Less than five years ago, the evangelical journal *Christian Scholars Review*, published quarterly by a coalition of such institutions as Wheaton College, Calvin College, and Gordon College, carried an article defending abortion-on-demand written by Virginia Mollenkott, an evangelical whose radical feminist views have become well-known in academic evangelical circles and which we will encounter again in chapter 3.[12]

Mollenkott began her article by insisting that the right to kill a fetus "as a last resort" is an indispensable part of what counts as "justice" for women in the late twentieth century. The words, "as a last resort," are Mollenkott's way of asking women, please, to consider other alternatives. But when push comes to shove, Mollenkott leaves no doubt that she believes it is up to the woman to decide whether the fetus lives or dies. Mollenkott's support for every woman's right to abortion extends even to its use as a form of birth control.

In an especially odd paragraph, Mollenkott states that "Pro-choice feminists do not devalue the fetus or even pit the rights of the woman against the rights of the fetus. Rather, we seek to support the woman's moral agency as she weighs the complex factors that must affect her decision, including the value of the fetus as potential human life, the quality of life that she could offer the fetus after its birth, the probable impact of that birth on the already existing web of her other relationships and responsibilities, and her own mental health and general well-being."[13]

If Mollenkott intends her words to be taken literally, she is claiming that *no* pro-abortion feminist devalues the fetus. Surely, this exaggerated statement is false. As one respondent to Mollenkott's article observed, "If killing a fetus by gruesome methods and disposing of the torn and charred remains like all other garbage is not 'devaluing' the fetus, what more can be done to devalue it?"[14] One must also object to the way in which Mollenkott describes every decision to put a fetus to death. It seems she would have us believe that totally selfish considerations never enter the minds of women contemplating abortion.

Mollenkott's major concern is how the decision to abort or not to abort affects only the woman. She notes that since the best birth control methods are effective only 90 percent of the time, every woman must retain the right to make birth control effective 100 percent of the time—by destroying the fetus. She expresses concern that unwanted children are often brought into the world to live miserable lives. The solution is to relieve the fetus of this possibility by simply killing it before birth. For Mollenkott, not even the option of adoption suggests that a pregnant woman has a moral responsibility to carry a fetus to term, if that woman decides it is in *her* interest to do otherwise.

A FEMINIST OBJECTION
TO THE PRO-ABORTION STANCE

One powerful case against the position Mollenkott defends appeared in a publication of an interesting organization called "Feminists for Life of America." The reader should note that the source of the arguments is not a right-wing organization or male-chauvinist fundamentalists. The arguments come from a group of card-carrying feminists who oppose abortion *on feminist principles*.

In a pamphlet titled "Abortion Does *Not* Liberate Woman," the feminist authors argue that the real beneficiaries of abortion are not women, but *men*! Instead of liberating women, the pamphlet maintains, abortion validates "the patriarchal world view which holds that women encumbered as they are by their reproductive capacity, are inferior to men."[15]

The pamphlet continues by arguing that "truly liberated women reject abortion because they reject the male world view that accepts violence as a legitimate solution to conflict. Rather than settling for mere equality—the right to contribute equally to the evil of the world—prolife feminists seek to transform society to create a world that reflects true feminist ideals."

When understood properly, the pamphlet goes on, "Feminism is . . . part of a larger philosophy that values all life. Feminists believe that all human beings have inherent worth and that this worth cannot be conferred or denied by another. True feminist thinking recognizes the interdependence of all living things and the responsibility we have for one another."

"Abortion is incompatible with this feminist vision," argues the pamphlet. Instead, "Abortion atomizes women. It pits them against their own children as competitors for the favors of the patriarchy. . . . Women who accept abortion have agreed to sacrifice their children for the convenience of a man's world."

This powerful argument asserts that violence and death have historically been the male's contribution to the human race. Women, on the other hand, are and should be the bearers and defenders of life. Pro-abortion feminists therefore are not defending feminine values; they are repudiating them and thus making their own contribution to the ongoing supremacy of the very patriarchy they profess to despise. Pro-abortion feminists, it concludes, are both anti-life and anti-women!

"Women who have been liberated from male thought patterns," the pamphlet continues, "refuse to participate in their own oppression and in the oppression of their children. They refuse to accept abortion, which denigrates the life-giving capacity of women. They strive instead to create a world that recognizes the moral superiority of maternal thinking and is, therefore, gentle, loving, nurturing, and pro-life. Every abortion frustrates this goal and perpetuates the patriarchy. Liberated women will not cooperate. They refuse abortion and all it represents."

Pro-abortion women are permitting men to evade all responsibility for male sexual conduct. Irresponsible men want their children aborted because it relieves them of undesired consequences, such as the obligation to support the children. "Women can be reduced to the status of a consumer item, which if 'broken' by pregnancy, can be 'fixed' by abortion."

Feminists for Life, therefore, is urging women to reflect on the true nature of feminism and womanhood. It calls on women to distinguish between a true feminism that defends life and a false feminism that not only supports death but, in doing so, helps promote the very patriarchy that it pretends to attack. "Women who agree to conform to the ideals of a world made by and for men are not liberated," the pamphlet contends. "They have merely altered their roles within the patriarchy."

Other publications available from Feminists for Life offer evidence that this line of thinking is not new. Another publication quotes, for example, from an 1878 letter from Elizabeth Cady Stanton to Julia Ward Howe stating, "When we consider that women are treated as property, it is degrading to women that we should treat our children as property to be disposed of as we see fit." Another publication quotes from the *Wheeling West Virginia Evening Standard* of November 17, 1875, in which Victoria Woodull argues that "every woman knows that if she were free, she would never . . . think of murdering [her child] before its birth."

The contemporary American obsession with the supposed "right" of women to kill their unborn children is a disgraceful, utterly self-centered demand that cannot be reconciled with the demands of a properly understood Christian ethic or with the demands of any proper understanding of feminism.

Ronald Sider—whose views on some related topics will receive more discussion later in this chapter—is surely correct when he argues that the problem of abortion results from "a secular individualism that makes the self-interest of the individual the highest value. By their sexual irresponsibility and failure to share fairly in the burdens of child care and parenting, many men have placed their individual selfish concerns above the rights of children, women and the larger community."[16]

What we find, then, in the defense of abortion by secular feminists is "the same destructive, individualistic selfishness," set in a context in which they appeal to the "very individualism which has long led many men to trample on the needs of children and the larger community. The solution surely is for both men and women to abandon secular individualism and refuse to place self above all others."[17]

What led us into the final stages of this discussion was

the realization that radical gender-feminism cannot tolerate any restraint, voluntary or otherwise, on a woman's reproductive powers. In such a context, no arguments or reasons could possibly persuade a gender-feminist to oppose abortion because the fetus has a right to life. Whether extreme Christian feminists like Virginia Mollenkott think of themselves as gender-feminists is less important than the fact that their reasoning about abortion touches all bases of the gender-feminist's position.

Cannot evangelical feminists feel any moral obligations toward the innocent unborn in the penumbra of the biblical ethic? Can they not feel the force and power of the Feminists for Life arguments that the pro-abortion stance is a betrayal of a true feminism that relieves sexually irresponsible males of the consequences of their behavior? Must they ignore the fact that this perpetuates the very patriarchy that feminists want everyone to believe they oppose? Some of the gender-feminists have turned their beliefs into a veritable ideology that goes beyond reason into a mystical, religious stance. But surely the Christian community has a right to expect that Christian feminists be more sensitive to the moral plight of the most important form of life over which we have control, the lives of unborn human babies.

THE "CONSISTENTLY PRO-LIFE" MOVEMENT

Earlier we noticed strong statements defending the unborn that were written by Ronald J. Sider. The pro-life cause is often thought of as the province of people belonging to the conservative right. For a number of years, however, Dr. Sider has been the strongest proponent of the pro-life position among people usually identified within the evangelical left. Pro-life Christians of all persuasions owe Sider much appreciation for all that he has done to arouse the interest of other representatives of the evangelical left in the pro-life cause.

As appreciative as pro-life supporters may be, Sider's efforts have not been without controversy. With each passing year, his representation of the pro-life cause has become increasingly mixed with a more extensive agenda that he describes as being consistently pro-life. Since the appearance of a 1987 book he edited, entitled *Completely Pro-Life*, Sider has worked hard to form a coalition of pro-life Protestants and Catholics who support liberal social programs. His cause has also sought to harness support from left-wing opponents of America's military and defense programs.

The consistently pro-life movement gets much of its energy from opposing what many have referred to as America's "killing fields": the hospitals and abortion clinics where the lives of one-and-a-half million fetuses are snuffed out each year. The movement then channels that energy and moral fervor to traditional liberal social and political causes. If you are really pro-life, its adherents argue, then you will act on behalf of other life-related issues. These other issues are closely aligned with the concerns of the political left.

Evaluation of the Consistently Pro-Life Movement

Basic to the position under investigation is the claim that abortion is only one way in which a pro-life stance is challenged. The consistently pro-life position criticizes the majority of the pro-life movement for inconsistency. Its supporters applaud the pro-life advocates for supporting the rights of the unborn. But why, the consistently pro-life position asks, do other pro-life supporters ignore the threats that cigarettes, drugs, nuclear weapons, and electric chairs pose to life?

After Dr. Sider gets pro-life supporters on the right thinking about additional dimensions of defending life, he turns to people on the left and asks, "Why do so many liberal and radical activists champion nuclear disarmament to protect the sanctity of human life and then defend the destruction of one-and-a-half million unborn American babies each year? Are 'sexual freedom' and affluent lifestyles finally more important than helpless, inconvenient babies?"[18]

In this way, Sider presents himself as somewhere in the middle of America's social and political strife. While he agrees with the left's stand on disarmament and social issues, he criticizes their inconsistency when they fail to extend humanitarian concern to the unborn. Sider applauds the commitment of the right to defending the unborn but criticizes their refusal to extend their concern for life to what he thinks are equally important pro-life positions.

Several months before the 1988 presidential and congressional election, Sider's movement published a thirty-two-page magazine titled *JustLife/88*. The attractive magazine included articles by such authors as Billy Graham, Joseph Bernardin (Roman Catholic cardinal of Chicago), and Roberta Hestenes (president of Eastern College), among others. Also included were advertisements for the latest books on liberal political issues, along with other ads inviting readers to join Sider's Evangelicals for Social Action and a Roman Catholic organization called Pax Christi.

JustLife/88 stressed that the consistently pro-life movement regards justice as a "seamless garment." Once the various segments of the consistently pro-life agenda have been identified, the magazine proposed, they are inseparable. In the words of the Frank Sinatra song, "You can't have one without the other." The catch was that, with the exception of opposition to abortion, the magazine's agenda was essentially indistinguishable from the typical, well-known objectives of the New Left.

JustLife/88 argued for a "wholistic vision" of things, calling on pro-life Americans to evaluate the votes of every member of Congress in terms of his or her fidelity to three major groups of issues: abortion, the nuclear arms race, and what was ambiguously referred to as "economic justice." A number of other issues—also part of the "seamless garment"—were present in the background: capital punishment, the environment, racism, and sexism.

At the end of the magazine, readers found a scorecard with

numbers showing how well various congressmen and senators had supported fifteen issues identified by the magazine's editors as reflective of consistently pro-life convictions. The senators' feelings about JustLife's version of economic justice were reflected by five Senate votes. Each of these concerned amendments offered by well-known liberal Democrats Howard Metzenbaum, Daniel Patrick Moynihan, Edward Kennedy, and Paul Simon. The proposed amendments dealt with the allocation of funds for a variety of social programs, as well as withholding money from the Strategic Defense Initiative, from the Nicaraguan contras, or from other defense issues. If a senator voted with the liberal Democrats, this—in the view of the magazine—proved that he was pro-life.

Another group of five votes reflected a senator's convictions on the nuclear arms race. Once again, the votes identified as the crucial test of a consistently pro-life position were representative of a typical liberal agenda.

A separate group of five votes dealt with abortion. But at this point, an embarrassing irony appeared. Most of the Senate liberals, whose votes on economic justice and nuclear disarmament had pleased the magazine's editors, voted *in favor of abortion*; they voted *against* life! This produced an embarrassing conclusion. Because liberal senators like Edward Kennedy, Howard Metzenbaum, and Alan Cranston voted for the ten liberal positions on "economic justice" and disarmament, they were assured of a score of 67 percent, *even though they voted against all of the recommended curbs on abortion*. However, conservative senators who voted the way the magazine's editors wanted them to on the abortion issue but not on the ten liberal issues would score just 33 percent.

By this final tally, *JustLife/88* was advising Christians to vote for the most pro-abortion members of the U.S. Senate. It also created the impression that Christians should vote against politically conservative senators, even though they were consistently opposed to abortion.

A similar paradox appeared in the magazine's scorecard for members of the U.S. House. As Richard John Neuhaus observed, "In the House of Representatives, denizens of the leftmost ideological fever swamps and relentless champions of abortion (e.g., Ron Dellums of California, George Crockett of Michigan, and Ted Weiss of New York) get generally favorable ratings, while many advocates of the unborn are given failing grades. The highly prejudiced scorecard rates Congressman Henry Hyde of Illinois as an opponent of life 60% of the time."[19]

Neuhaus went on to complain, "The entire logic of the election guide is that a candidate's vote for government day care, for example, cancels out his vote against protecting the unborn."[20] The inescapable consequence of this bizarre document is simply this: *If the candidates favored by JustLife are elected, it will guarantee an overwhelming pro-abortion majority in the United States Congress.* Obviously, there are many people who would welcome that."[21] Incredibly, many of these pro-abortion people would be considered friends of the unborn by the JustLife supporters!

Neuhaus argued that the whole disaster required an apology from those who perpetrated "the arrogantly wrongheaded fiasco that is JustLife."[22] The very structure of the JustLife project "relativizes, trivializes, and finally neutralizes the question of abortion." Therefore, we must, Neuhaus insists, "look elsewhere for an explanation of why people who say they are profoundly committed to the protection of the unborn endorse a program that, were it successful, would assure the triumph of pro-abortion forces in American political life."[23] When we recall that JustLife equates its own political agenda with the will of God, the result, Neuhaus insists, "is as gross a display of moral arrogance as anything witnessed in recent American history."[24]

The debate over JustLife and the consistently pro-life movement generated enough heat to produce a lengthy exchange in the

July 14, 1989 issue of *Christianity Today*. The task of critiquing JustLife in this debate went to Charles E. White, a professor at an evangelical college. White pointed to the confusion between ends and means as one place where he thought the JustLife people went wrong. Even when the correct ends or goals are pursued, the selection of the wrong means assures that the goals will remain unreachable.

JustLife is right to say, White argues, "that God's will is plain in its opposition to abortion, economic injustice, and war. The elimination of these three wrongs is clearly God's goal for our society. Saving lives by ending abortion, poverty, and the threat of nuclear war is certainly an end that God wants us to reach."[25]

The problem, however, is that JustLife "forgets that having the right end is only part of the answer. The issue is more complex. In the real world of politics, we have to have the correct means to achieve our good ends. Good intentions are not enough."[26] Few of us know any Americans who have evil intentions when it comes to things like peace and poverty. Everyone says they want to help end poverty and promote peace. The question, White insists, is seldom about ends; it is about proper means to those ends.

But when we enter the arena to do battle over abortion, the people on opposite sides *are* promoting opposing goals. Pro-abortion people demand the right to destroy fetal life; pro-life people seek to save life. Furthermore, the ambiguities and complexities that make correct decisions in the social and political arena so difficult do not apply in the matter of abortion. "God's Word makes it clear that He wants society to protect weak, innocent, and defenseless people," White argues.[27] Biblical passages such as Exodus 21:22-25, Psalm 139:13-16, Proverbs 24:11-12, Jeremiah 1:5, and Luke 1:15 teach that the unborn child is a human person whose life is valuable in God's eyes.

So when it comes to the issue of abortion, there can be little doubt where the battle lines are to be drawn or where people who claim to be Christians should be standing. But the issues of economic justice and peace are different in the sense that while sincere Christians ought to agree about their desirability as ends, we may nonetheless disagree over the best means to achieve those ends. This leads White to claim that "JustLife is not being biblically faithful when it identifies one particular political position as the God-ordained means to achieve these godly ends. Here it is going beyond the Word of God into areas where God has not authoritatively spoken. It is making conclusions it has reached on its own and passing them off as God's inerrant revelation."[28]

JustLife's confusion over the means-ends issue resulted in political recommendations that are counterproductive, White argues. Their congressional scorecard implied that the votes of pro-abortion liberals like Howard Metzenbaum of Ohio and Alan Cranston of California are twice as pleasing to God as the votes of a pro-life senator like William Armstrong of Colorado (now retired) or a pro-life congressman like Henry Hyde of Illinois.

Obviously stung by some of these criticisms, Dr. Sider tried to play down the blatant bias of *JustLife/88* and denied that his movement sides with one particular political position—a claim that people familiar with his organization found disingenuous. Sider did admit that the use of percentages in *JustLife/88* was a minor mistake that some readers misused to reach conclusions that the magazine's editors did not intend. It boggles my mind to think that the editors didn't know what they were implying and did not intend the percentages to lead readers to vote for liberal candidates. However, Sider promised that future issues would avoid the mistakes of the first issue. With these promises in mind, it is instructive to see what Sider's group did in its next publication, *JustLife/90*.

JustLife/90 appeared in time to influence votes in the congressional elections of 1990. It included an essay by long-time supporter of the left-wing evangelical magazine *Sojourners*,

Senator Mark Hatfield, along with articles by several politically liberal Roman Catholics. But once again, its focus was the new scorecard for Senate and House candidates.

The 1990 issue differed from its predecessor in at least two ways. First, percentages were not used as a measurement of congressional votes. Second, the identification of key votes (reduced to four votes each on "economic justice," abortion, and nuclear arms) appeared to have been choosen more carefully, so as not to reflect quite so badly on politicians like Senator Hatfield, who supports the JustLife organization.

Unfortunately, a careful examination of the test votes on economic and nuclear issues reflects the same problems noted in connection with *JustLife/88*. The identified issues failed to reflect sincere evangelical disagreements on the means-ends issue.

For example, one vote in the area of economic justice hinged on support for the more extreme minimum wage bill favored by congressional liberals. This ignored considerable evidence offered by many economists that minimum wage laws do not help the poor. In the long run, these economic experts argue, such laws actually harm the poor by making unskilled workers less employable.[29] Only someone pushing a particular political agenda would select a liberal minimum wage bill as a reflection of God's will and as a test of genuine concern for the poor.

Another extremely complex issue that *JustLife/90* oversimplified is the matter of military aid to El Salvador. Obviously, there have been deplorable human rights abuses by all sides in the Salvadoran conflict. Although listening to the left, one would think the abuses were never perpetrated by the communist rebels. Regrettably, *JustLife/90* took the extreme left position that undermined any real hope of ending the Marxist insurgency, of weakening the power of corrupt government officials, and of strengthening democracy in El Salvador. Many critics believe the far left in the United States either wanted the Marxist rebels to win, thus producing another Nicaragua, or at least wanted them to have significant power in a new government, thus raising the hope of a more gradual Marxist takeover. These claims are disputed by the evangelical left, of course. But that is precisely my point here: Why select this highly controversial vote as a test of congressional morality and honor? It makes one wonder once again if a hidden agenda was at work in the JustLife scorecard.

Unfortunately, every one of *JustLife/90*'s test votes on economic justice and the nuclear issue was highly controversial and concerned issues on which good and honorable people can disagree. But such legitimate disagreement was ignored by the editors of the *JustLife* magazine who appear to have set their tests up in ways that best serve their own political agenda.[30]

CONCLUSION

This brings us back to the major critiques of the evangelical feminists and the "consistently pro-life" position.

We saw how the position of many evangelical feminists ultimately leads to a denial of the rights of the unborn. Through interesting rhetoric that sounds similar to that of radical gender-feminists, some evangelicals have abandoned the traditional pro-life position of the evangelical majority. In its place some of them now support even abortion-on-demand—a position that clearly cannot be reconciled with a biblical ethic.

We have also seen that one unfortunate result of the consistently pro-life movement is that the cause of the unborn often gets lost in the shuffle. What started as an attempt to make the pro-life movement more consistent turns out to be bad news for the unborn, at least as far as congressional voting is concerned.

Recommendations to vote against pro-life candidates and support pro-abortion candidates are not, I suggest, good examples of a consistently pro-life position. To repeat an earlier quote from Richard John Neuhaus, himself once an ardent representative of the left, the JustLife project "relativizes, trivializes, and finally neutralizes the question of abortion."[31]

Charles E. White has, therefore, hit the target when he writes that "JustLife should stop its talk about a 'consistent ethic of life' and make it clear that there is only one issue facing our government where Americans openly disagree about the ends we are trying to reach: abortion. God's will is clear on the ends and means [in this case], and rejecting God's will in this matter is such a moral monstrosity that it dwarfs all other squabbling about means."[32] What this means, White continues, is, "The people in JustLife should stop trying to divert the concern, energy, and money of committed Christians away from the God-given ends of the prolife movement and into side issues relating to human means. They should give priority to the one issue where there is a clearly defined method of fulfilling God's will, and then, with other Christians, seek his mind about how to do his will in other areas."[33]

It is clear, then, that the seamless garment of the consistently pro-life movement tears apart at a critical seam, compromising support for the cause of the unborn. Christians who are truly consistently pro-life will not sacrifice the unborn on the altar of politics.

Chapter Two

THE CONTROVERSY OVER WOMEN LEADERS IN THE CHURCH

P ossibly only a twentieth-century Rip van Winkle, asleep somewhere since the end of World War II, would be unaware of the heated debate going on over the role of women in society. Within the Christian church, this debate centers around whether women should occupy leadership roles, such as pastor or elder. For those who never consider the teaching of the Bible or allow it to inform their beliefs, the issue is cut and dried. Such a position is often predictably liberal, and its contribution to the debate not terribly interesting.

The debate gets interesting when this disagreement is examined within the company of Christians who take the Bible as the authoritative Word of God. It is *this* debate that we will examine in this chapter. Many Christians assert that the Bible clearly teaches that women are not to assume roles in which they have teaching and/or leadership duties over men. But equally sincere Christians who also yield to the authority of Scripture disagree. When the Bible is understood correctly, they argue, nothing prohibits women from serving as pastors or in other leadership capacities. In fact, there is plenty of biblical support for women serving as church leaders, they say.

FIVE POSITIONS DISTINGUISHED

Whenever an especially complex problem is tackled, it is often wise, when possible, to begin with an identification of the major positions honorable people hold. In the case presently before us, it is important to distinguish five different viewpoints. The following diagram identifies the labels I have given these positions:

Anti-Christian Feminism	Anti-Evangelical Feminism	Evangelical Feminism (critical view of Bible)	Biblical Equalitarianism (high view of Bible)	Traditional Non-Feminism

Following established custom, the more conservative positions appear on the right side of the diagram. As one moves from right to left, the viewpoints get increasingly less conservative until we reach the most radical position available, which I have called *Anti-Christian Feminism.*

Traditional Non-Feminism

Strict traditionalists hold that the Bible teaches that men and women must always exist in a hierarchical relationship in which men have authority over women. According to this view, male headship is God's plan in both the home and the church. It is God's will always and everywhere that women not occupy positions in which they have authority over men or preach to men. Most traditionalists hasten to add, however, that inequality of function doesn't imply inequality of essence. In other words, women and men are equal as human beings. The strict traditionalist insists upon distinctions of function or role, rather than differences of essence.

Variations of this traditionalist view may be found in a number of books, including: Stephen Clark, *Man and Woman in Christ* (Ann Arbor, MI: Servant, 1980); Susan Foh, *Women and the Word of God* (Philadelphia, PA: Presbyterian and

Reformed, 1980); George Knight, *New Testament Teaching on the Role Relationship of Men and Women* (Grand Rapids, MI: Baker, 1977); and Charles C. Ryrie, *The Role of Women in the Church* (Chicago, IL: Moody, 1970). The most extensive and impressive treatment of this position to appear in recent years is *Recovering Biblical Manhood & Womanhood*, John Piper and Wayne Grudem, eds. (Wheaton, IL: Crossway, 1991). I'll say more about this book shortly.

Biblical Equalitarianism

I have selected the two words for this position carefully. There is merit, I think, in distinguishing between feminists and equalitarians. Both assert that women may properly fill leadership roles in the church. But recently, the word *feminism* has accumulated a lot of negative baggage, at least for some people. Those who take the position I call *biblical equalitarianism* deserve better than to be saddled with the negative connotations often associated with feminism. For one thing, some forms of feminism suggest a mood of militancy that does not always characterize the people I'll discuss in this section.

What makes these people *biblical* equalitarians is the fact that—unlike the people who advocate the third position we'll be examining—they accept without question the inerrancy of the Bible. Biblical equalitarians affirm without reservation the essential doctrines of historic Christianity and hold a high view of Scripture in the sense that they refuse to defend their position on female leadership in ways that impute error to the Bible.

Biblical equalitarianism is set apart from all types of feminism by its conviction that nothing in the Bible, when interpreted properly, teaches that women are second-class citizens, whether in regard to Christian service or any other aspect of humanness. A biblical equalitarian approaches all of the so-called "problem texts" without impugning the infallibility or the authority of Scripture. Moreover, this position does not entail any commitment with regard to additional issues, such as inclusive language. Representatives of this group may or may not endorse inclusive language when referring to human beings; they usually repudiate efforts to use inclusive language (for example, feminine pronouns) with respect to God.

Hence, biblical equalitarianism does not deny any essential Christian beliefs, does not impute error to the Bible, and does not argue for inclusive language in references to God.

Biblical equalitarians also recognize that they do not have to oppose all hierarchies in male-female relationships. There is certainly nothing wrong, they admit, with hierarchical relationships based upon superior experience or qualifications. They would consider it silly to oppose the typical parent-child relationship, for example. Biblical equalitarians do resist hierarchical relationships when they are based on irrelevant considerations.

Some of the books that represent the biblical equalitarian position include: Gilbert Bilezikian, *Beyond Sex Roles* (Grand Rapids, MI: Baker, 1985); Mary Evans, *Women in the Bible* (Downers Grove, IL: InterVarsity, 1983); and Patricia Gundry, *Woman Be Free* (Grand Rapids, MI: Zondervan, 1977). Some think that Letha Scanzoni's and Nancy Hardesty's book, *All We're Meant to Be* (Waco, TX: Word, 1974), fits under the category of biblical equalitarianism.

Evangelical Feminism
As many readers know, the Christian church contains defenders of female church leadership who, while orthodox on most essential Christian beliefs, think that the Bible is wrong in what it teaches on *this* issue. The major difference between what I call biblical equalitarians and evangelical feminists is that the latter feel constrained to criticize the Bible in order to defend their position about women.

A well-known example of this approach is Fuller Seminary professor Paul Jewett's book *Man as Male and Female.* Jewett resolved the problem of what he saw as a contradiction between feminism and the teaching of the apostle Paul by rejecting the latter.[1] Robert K. Johnston summarized Jewett's view: "Rather than struggle to understand the cultural background of the text and the alternative meanings suggested by recent historic-grammatical research, Jewett is content to judge the text as reflecting Paul's rabbinic conditioning and disregard it. It is as if Paul was a split-person, unable to resolve his conflicts of sexism and Christian liberty in a consistent manner."[2]

As far back as 1976, Virginia Mollenkott, who described herself as an evangelical, came right out and stated that "there are flat contradictions between some of [Paul's] theological arguments and his own doctrines and behavior."[3] She believed that Paul's writings about women were the record of his battles with his earlier rabbinical training, which included the belief that women should be subordinated to men.[4]

It is clear, then, that the major difference between biblical equalitarians and evangelical feminists is their stance with regard to the Bible. Biblical equalitarians are committed to a high view of Scripture, refusing to base their defense of equalitarianism upon criticism of the Bible. While evangelical feminists tend to support other essentials of Christian orthodoxy, their view of Scripture is disappointingly and often uncritically liberal.

Anti-Evangelical Feminism

We should not be surprised that there are feminists who—while committed to their own version of Christianity—hold theological positions so unmistakably liberal as to place them outside the evangelical camp. The view of Scripture held by this group of feminists falls far below what would be acceptable to evangelicals in any of the three groups noted thus far: traditional non-feminists, biblical equalitarians, and evangelical feminists.

For *anti-evangelical feminists*, the Bible contains God's words but in its entirety must never be identified as the Word of God. The portions of the Bible that supposedly teach patriarchy (male domination) are, in their thinking, disqualified from being divine revelation. In other words, the Bible is accepted as divine revelation when it supports the convictions of the anti-evangelical feminist. But when it does not, that fact alone is sufficient to disqualify those portions of Scripture.

I will say much more about anti-evangelical feminists in the following chapter. For now, it is sufficient to indicate some representatives of the movement: Elizabeth Schussler Fiorenza, *In Memory of Her* (New York: Crossroad, 1983); Sallie McFague, *Metaphorical Theology* (Philadelphia, PA: Fortress, 1982); Rosemary Radford Reuther, *Sexism and God-Talk: Toward a Feminist Theology* (Boston, MA: Beacon, 1983); and Letty Russell, *Human Liberation in a Feminist Perspective: A Theology* (Philadelphia, PA: Westminster, 1974).

Anti-Christian Feminism

As respected theologian Donald Bloesch describes them, the post-Christian or *anti-Christian feminists* "regard Christianity as incurably patriarchal and sexist and . . . therefore opt for a new religion, one that proves to be a form of nature mysticism."[5]

The radical feminists who are theologically liberal or anti-evangelical abandon the unquestioned authority of the Bible. Because they believe patriarchy and a male-bias pervade the Bible, they think it cannot be viewed as revelation. The center of revelation must instead be the experience of women or communities of women who are united in their quest for liberation from patriarchal domination.

But anti-Christian feminists abandon more than the Bible's authority. Anti-Christian feminists believe that women must reject the whole of the Christian faith if they are ever to experience liberation. The post-Christian feminists in view here believe they must rename God from the perspective of their new and radical spiritual experience—an experience that has been freed from any male influence. These religious experiences may and often do include witchcraft and lesbianism. They find "Mother Goddess" to be a much more satisfying way of conceptualizing the Divine Being. Not surprisingly, their newfound goddess religion provides added impetus to their interest in lesbianism and pantheism.[6]

Several representatives of anti-Christian feminism started out as theologically liberal Christian feminists, the group I call anti-evangelical feminists. Mary Daly, author of *Beyond God the Father, Toward a Philosophy of Women's Liberation* (Boston, MA: Beacon, 1973), is an ex-Roman Catholic. Carol Christ, author of *Laughter of Aphrodite, Reflections on a Journey to the Goddess* (San Francisco, CA: Harper and Row, 1987), was a liberal Protestant. As we will see in the next chapter, radical anti-Christian feminists have made it clear that the important debate in Western religion is not the status of women's rights, but rather the true understanding of the nature of God.

EVALUATING EVANGELICAL POSITIONS

I have already explained that what interests me in this debate is the give-and-take between traditional non-feminists and biblical equalitarians. Since the amount of space that can be devoted to any single issue in this book is limited, I will discuss anti-evangelical and anti-Christian feminists in the following chapter.

Evangelical Feminism

Our previous glance at the views of feminists Virginia Mollenkott and Paul Jewett revealed the ease with which they dismissed New Testament statements that were in apparent conflict with their feminism. Mollenkott has appeared unwilling even to consider the possibility that the apostle Paul's statements about women may have been culturally misunderstood. Instead, she opted for the easy way out, denigrating Paul's statements as reflections of his human limitations and the cultural conditioning of his rabbinical training. Robert Johnston, clearly disappointed with Mollenkott's sub-biblical position, regrets that she "let the 'good reasons' of feminism judge the Pauline texts." Instead of placing "the insights of contemporary society in dialogue with Scripture and tradition in a way that maintains Biblical authority, she has compromised the sole authority of Scripture by qualifying it from feminist perspectives."[7]

The willingness of Jewett, Mollenkott, and other self-described evangelical feminists to give their convictions priority over the Bible is a decidedly non-evangelical position. The question such feminists need to face squarely is whether they will allow their feminist views to stand in judgment over Scripture or whether they will subordinate their feminist convictions to the authority of Scripture and the beliefs of historic Christianity based upon it. Once "evangelicals" begin to denigrate Scripture passages that fail to accord with their preconceived opinions, they cease to be evangelicals!

The kind of theological drift that can be detected in evangelical feminists is difficult to understand when one realizes the options open to them had they chosen the path taken by biblical equalitarians. Many evangelical feminists evidence little interest in exploring whether Paul's statements about women have been understood correctly.

Several years ago, the California seminary where Paul Jewett had taught for many years hired a New Testament professor from another school to teach a part-time course on the pastoral epistles. Since this scholar was a traditionalist, his handling of the Pauline texts that are central to the dispute favored the view that women are not to serve as pastors. Several feminists who were taking his class were outraged and complained to the seminary administration, who promptly called the visiting professor on the carpet for his alleged insensitivity and dogmatism. The response of the professor is worth remembering. "Let me see if I have this right," he said. "For years, this evangelical seminary defended one of its professors when he argued that Paul was *wrong* about this particular issue. And now, this seminary is criticizing me for arguing that Paul was *right!*" The professor was drawing attention to the fact that this is an odd stance for a seminary to take when it wishes to be viewed as evangelical.

One central, nonnegotiable essential of evangelicalism is its high view of Scripture and its conviction that the Bible is without error. The evangelical feminists make it clear that they have abandoned this nonnegotiable doctrine. It's important to understand their view; but they leave us with a key question: How can we continue to regard them as evangelicals?

Biblical Equalitarianism
The phrase *give-and-take* is an apt description of the serious and important debate presently occurring between traditional non-feminists and biblical equalitarians. That phrase sets the tone for much that I say in the rest of this chapter. In this section, I will note a new aggressiveness on the part of evangelicals supportive of biblical equalitarianism. In the following section, I'll focus on some counter moves from the traditionalists. In subsequent sections, I'll examine some of the major strengths and weaknesses of these two evangelical positions.

In the April 9, 1990 issue of *Christianity Today*, an organization called "Christians for Biblical Equality" published a two-page advertisement titled "Men, Women and Biblical Equality."[8] Many of the people who signed the manifesto are evangelicals who fall into the group I've called biblical equalitarianism; that is, they support female equality but would never stoop to a critical view of the Bible in order to justify their position.[9] Among the biblical equalitarians signing the document were Bill Hybels, prominent evangelical pastor and author; Kenneth Kantzer, for many years dean of Trinity Evangelical Divinity School and a past editor of *Christianity Today*; Stanley Gundry of Zondervan Publishing House; the late F. F. Bruce, famed British New Testament scholar; Richard Longenecker, another knowledgeable New Testament scholar;

and Richard Mouw, the new president of Fuller Theological Seminary.

The main claim of the advertisement is that "the Bible teaches the full equality of men and women in Creation and in Redemption (Gen. 1:26-28; 2:23; 5:1-2; 1 Cor. 11:11-12; Gal. 3:13, 28; 5:1)." The manifesto goes on to point out that "the Bible teaches that at Pentecost the Holy Spirit came on men and women alike. Without distinction, the Holy Spirit indwells women and men, and sovereignly distributes gifts without preference as to gender (Acts 2:1-21; 1 Cor. 12:7, 11; 14:31)."

According to the manifesto, "The Bible teaches that both women and men are called to develop their spiritual gifts and to use them as stewards of the grace of God (1 Peter 4:10-11). Both men and women are divinely gifted and empowered to minister to the whole Body of Christ, under His authority (Acts 1:14; 18:6; 21:9; Rom. 16:1-7, 12-13, 15; Phil. 4:2-3; Col. 4:15; see also Mark 15:40-41; 16:-1-7; Luke 8:1-13; John 20:17-18 . . .)."

Later the manifesto cites a number of New Testament texts that teach that "women as well as men exercise the prophetic, priestly and royal functions." These passages include Acts 2:17-18, 21:9; 1 Corinthians 11:5; 1 Peter 2:9-10; and Revelation 1:6, 5:10.

The sections I've quoted constitute only a small part of the entire two-page advertisement, but they're sufficient to indicate a major line of the biblical equalitarian's argument. According to this view, the New Testament records a number of instances in which women engaged in ministry: Acts 2:17, 18:26; Romans 16:1-7; 1 Timothy 3:11. Accounting for these texts is a problem for the strict traditionalist.[10] The challenge for the biblical equalitarian is accounting for other texts that appear to place restrictions on a ministry-role for women.

Problem Texts for the Equalitarian
Obviously, certain Scripture passages create problems for the

equalitarian position. Two of the most frequently cited are 1 Corinthians 14:33-36 and 1 Timothy 2:9-15. The first passage says,

> For God is not a God of disorder but of peace.
> As in all the congregations of the saints, women should remain silent in the churches. They are not allowed to speak, but must be in submission, as the Law says. If they want to inquire about something, they should ask their own husbands at home; for it is disgraceful for a woman to speak in the church.

These statements clearly settle the issue for many Christians. What the equalitarian says in response is that we should proceed more slowly. For one thing, we want to take pains that our interpretation of this passage does not contradict other New Testament material.

Suppose the equalitarians are right, they contend, and some women in the New Testament did exercise teaching authority, as in the passages noted earlier. Then the traditionalists' reading of 1 Corinthians 14:33-36 is difficult to reconcile with those other verses. It is also hard to reconcile with Galatians 3:28 which, equalitarians contend, is Paul's definitive statement on male-female relationships. The verse reads, "There is neither Jew nor Greek, slave nor free, male nor female, for you are all one in Christ Jesus." Outside of Christ, the cultures of Paul's day discriminated among people on all of these grounds, but Paul taught that our new relationship to God through Christ creates new relationships among believers. While pagan cultures continued to discriminate on the basis of gender, Paul taught that this was no longer permitted.[11]

But the killer so far as this passage goes, equalitarians contend, is the fact that Paul stated in 1 Corinthians 14:5,13 that *everyone* in Corinth may speak in church. These verses refer to prophesying and praying in the church.

For all these reasons and more, equalitarians argue, Paul must be doing something more than simply forbidding all women to speak or teach in any congregation. There are good reasons, therefore, to believe that special problems existed in the Corinthian church that led Paul to state that whenever those conditions or similar ones exist in any church, *then* women should not speak.

Well, then, what were those local conditions? That is not easy to say, equalitarians admit. Perhaps women in the Corinthian church were disrupting worship; possibly women in the church were teaching some serious error. But whether we're able to identify the precise problem or not is less relevant than the suggestion that Paul was attempting to deal with a local problem.[12]

This line of argument is *totally* different from suggesting that Paul mistakenly allowed facets of his own rabbinical training or cultural influences to distort his understanding of the role of women in the church. As W. Ward Gasque explained, "The danger for the church in Paul's day lay in the exact opposite direction from the church in our day, that is, there was the danger that it might press the principle of Christian freedom too far."[13] What this means is that the sort of legalism found in some Christian circles then and now was not the problem in Corinth. The Corinthians instead had a propensity toward unrestrained libertinism, to the extent that Paul evidently felt they might compromise the purpose and testimony of true Christian liberty.

Gasque's approach views Paul's teaching about women as similar to Paul's teaching about Christians eating meat that had been offered to idols (Romans 14). First-century Christians frequently had to contend with the fact that the only meat available for consumption had been "blessed" in some pagan ritual. Some Christians were offended when other believers ate meat that had been offered to false gods. In Romans 14, Paul made it clear that conduct in such cases was a matter of Christian liberty. There was nothing sinful about a Christian's eating this kind of meat; but there was plenty wrong when Christians judged other believers who did. Yet Paul's argument in this regard was like a two-sided coin. On the other side, he criticized believers who engaged in any practice, however innocent, that led weaker Christians to stumble.

Since God is the ultimate judge, Christians should avoid judging others who exercise their liberty in Christ differently. But we should also avoid doing anything that would lead weaker brothers and sisters astray. This latter reason led Paul to the decision that he would avoid eating meat. "Let us therefore," he wrote, "make every effort to do what leads to peace and to mutual edification. Do not destroy the work of God for the sake of food. All food is clean, but it is wrong for a man to eat anything that causes someone else to stumble. It is better not to eat meat or drink wine or to do anything else that will cause your brother to fall" (Romans 14:19-21).

In cases when a morally neutral act such as eating meat offered to idols might cause misunderstanding, Paul would approve restraints on the behavior. Similarly, in local circumstances when a woman's teaching or speaking in church would result in misunderstanding and harm to the cause of the gospel, Paul would approve restraints, as in 1 Corinthians 14. But in neither case, equalitarians argue, can we infer a universal or trans-cultural norm.

To think otherwise about Pauline claims that appear to restrict women from leadership roles, equalitarians contend, would contradict not only Galatians 3:28 but also the New Testament's approving reports of the ministry of women (Acts 2:17, 18:26; Romans 16:1-7; 1 Timothy 3:11): "There is neither Jew nor Greek, slave nor free, male nor female, for you are all one in Christ Jesus."

Thus, verses such as 1 Corinthians 14:34 should be understood as *local* restrictions that were necessary for the sake of Christian testimony under specific conditions in specific places. And whenever similar problems arose in any other church, then Paul would command that there too, women should remain silent. Understood correctly, nothing Paul says in 1 Corinthians 14 precludes women exercising leadership roles in the church—or so say the biblical equalitarians.

First Timothy 2:9-15 is a notoriously difficult passage to interpret, even for traditionalists who regard it as the strongest text for their position. The passage states,

> I also want women to dress modestly, with decency
> and propriety, not with braided hair or gold or pearls or
> expensive clothes, but with good deeds, appropriate for
> women who profess to worship God.
> A woman should learn in quietness and full sub-
> mission. I do not permit a woman to teach or to have
> authority over a man; she must be silent. For Adam
> was formed first, then Eve. And Adam was not the one
> deceived; it was the woman who was deceived and
> became a sinner. But women will be saved through
> childbirth—if they continue in faith, love and holiness
> with propriety.

The most puzzling verses in this passage are the ones dealing with Adam and Eve. What could they possibly have to do with Paul's command that women in the church in Ephesus must be silent? Even traditionalists are forced to admit that Paul is alluding to conditions in the Ephesian church that are hard for those of us in the late twentieth century to get a handle on.

Scott McClelland, a biblical equalitarian, urges evangelicals to tread carefully when interpreting this passage. "Let us be cautious," he warns, "in assigning to this passage the normative force so often given to it by traditionalists."[14] His reason for saying this is, "The cultural background is ripe with pagan religious practices in Ephesus that emphasized the feminine aspect of deity to the exclusion of the masculine in many cases."[15]

Paul's very selective argument that appears to counteract other stated principles, and parallel passages that appear to indicate restrictions for the sake of propriety (Titus 2:4-5), should temper our universalizing these restrictions outside very similar contexts. There are too many unclear points for us to be completely sure about what Paul is specifically restricting.[16]

For McClelland, it is clear that everything Paul says in 1 Timothy 2 must be reconciled with Galatians 3:28. This leads him to say that "Paul's clearly enunciated principle of equality (Gal. 3:28) was evidently modified *only* when either the manner or the type of [women's] participation in church life had negative cultural implications (1 Cor. 11:14), or when a specific heretical problem involving women was involved (1 Tim. 2)."[17]

McClelland leaves so many details of 1 Timothy 2 untouched, that it is difficult to imagine too many equalitarians being satisfied with his account of the passage, much less traditionalists. A more ambitious attempt to deal with the problems in 1 Timothy 2 has been made by Bruce Barron.[18]

Barron maintains that Paul's reference to Adam and Eve is not an appeal to a timeless hierarchy of the sexes based upon the order in which they were created. Instead, he suggests, "1 Tim. 2:13-14 makes very good sense as a coherent counter-argument to a specific problem [in the Ephesian church]—namely, a false interpretation of Genesis by heretical women."[19] These women had come under the influence of certain gnostic-like arguments that account for the otherwise strange statements made by Paul.[20] One of those beliefs concerned a gnostic teaching that Eve's existence preceded Adam's. Coupled with the additional belief that Eve was intellectually superior to Adam, the heretical women in Ephesus could appeal to this precedent as a basis for their own self-appointed superiority.

Barron explains why Paul tells the women in Ephesus to be silent, why he refers to the creation order of Adam and Eve, and why he states that women will be saved through childbirth. In Barron's words,

> The gospel is struggling in Ephesus with gnostic influenced women trumpeting a feminist reinterpretation of Adam and Eve as precedent for their own spiritual primacy and authority. Puffed up by this interpretation, the women are ignoring both Timothy's authority as teacher and their own ethical responsibilities. In response Paul reasserts the Genesis version of the fall, draws attention to the inseparability of ethical behavior from true Christian spirituality, and urges Timothy to place women in subjection until the feminist threat to true doctrine has subsided. To reassure recalcitrant women, Paul promises that Eve's curse, though still valid, will not be as painful as they might fear.[21]

Even though Barron is a biblical equalitarian, he thinks it's important to see that "the limitations thus placed temporarily on genuinely gifted women are less harmful to the congregation than the confusion fostered by the existence of women leaders in this gnostic context would be."[22] He sees an interesting application of 1 Timothy 2 to our own time. We live in a day, Barron observes, "in which all too many women have brought the angry, divisive cultural baggage of radical feminism into their justifiable quest for a share of Church leadership. Perhaps, ironically, periods of feminist ideology are the times in which the Church does need to consider temporary limitations on women in leadership."[23]

How convincing are these equalitarian interpretations of their problem texts? That is hard to say. Perhaps the major obstacle to any resolution of this dispute between traditionalists and biblical equalitarians is the fact that representatives of both positions bring presuppositions to the table, which have an understandable influence on how they read the key biblical texts.

Problem Texts for Traditionalists

While the brief statement of traditionalism given earlier adequately set the stage for this chapter, it is time to amplify and modify it. Thoughtful traditionalists would likely object to any simple reduction of their position to the twin notions of traditionalism and hierarchism.

John Piper and Wayne Grudem, editors of *Recovering Biblical Manhood & Womanhood*, prefer *complementarianism* to *traditionalism* as the main designation of their view. The word *complementarianism* suggests, they write, "both equality and beneficial differences between men and women."[24] While I am sympathetic to their concern, the fact is that *traditionalism*, at least up to now, is the term encountered most frequently.

Piper, Grudem, and other contributors to their book also object to any emphasis upon some merely hierarchical relationship between men and women. Rather, they maintain, God has assigned different complementary roles to men and women both in the family and in the church. While God has important tasks for women within this complementary relationship, leadership is not one of them.

Equalitarians make much of the fact that women held positions of prominence in the Old Testament (Exodus 15:20, Numbers 12:2, Judges 4:4, 2 Chronicles 34:22). Moreover, they point out, Paul had many female coworkers. Twenty-nine people are mentioned in Romans 16, possibly ten of them women. Equalitarians think Junias, likely a woman, is mentioned in a way that appears to include her among the apostles. Traditionalists assume that equalitarians have the burden of proof, suggest that none of these cases constitutes proof, and conclude that equalitarians have failed to produce the proof.[25]

As we've seen, Galatians 3:28 occupies center stage in the equalitarian defense. It is interesting to see what traditionalists say about this text. Piper and Grudem assigned this task to S. Lewis Johnson, the senior pastor of Believers Chapel in

Dallas and a respected former professor of theology at both Dallas Theological Seminary and Trinity Evangelical Divinity School in Chicago.[26]

Johnson's major argument is that equalitarians have basically read their position into Paul's words. When Paul wrote that "there is neither Jew nor Greek, slave nor free, male nor female," he was saying only "that every believer in Christ inherits fully the Abrahamic promises by grace apart from legal works."[27] Thus, Johnson concludes,

> There is no reason to claim that Galatians 3:28 supports an egalitarianism of function in the church. It does plainly teach an egalitarianism of privilege in the covenantal union of believers in Christ. The Abrahamic promises . . . belong universally to the family of God. Questions of roles and functions in that body can only be answered by a consideration of other and later New Testament teaching.[28]

Will this interpretation of Galatians 3:28 be any more satisfying to equalitarians than their reading of 1 Timothy 2 is to traditionalists? Once again, it appears, the response people make to interpretations of these key but difficult texts reflects their earlier assumptions. Both sides insist that the burden of proof rests with the other position.

This shifting of the burden of proof to equalitarians is also apparent in the traditionalist handling of other problem texts. For example, Acts 18:26 seems to report that Priscilla taught Apollos. She is even mentioned before her husband, Aquilla. Does this not show that the early church permitted women to occupy a teaching position? Piper and Grudem respond first by assuming that equalitarians have the burden of proof in this matter. Once this assumption is made, they have little difficulty showing that the evidence does not support the equalitarian verdict. They write,

We are eager to affirm Priscilla as a fellow worker with Paul in Christ (Romans 16:30)! She and her husband were very influential in the church in Corinth (1 Corinthians 16:19) as well as Ephesus. We can think of many women in our churches today who are like Priscilla. Nothing in our understanding of Scripture says that when a husband and wife visit an unbeliever (or a confused believer or anyone else) the wife must be silent. It is easy for us to imagine the dynamics of such a discussion in which Priscilla contributes to the explanation and illustration of baptism in Jesus' name and the work of the Holy Spirit.[29]

This is about all any traditionalist can do with similar texts, such as Romans 16:7, which refers to Junias, whom equalitarians regard as a female apostle. But, traditionalists counter, how can we be certain that Junias was a woman? Since we cannot, the equalitarians base a highly significant claim on a shaky foundation.[30] For those who assume that equalitarians carry the burden of proof, such a reply will seem persuasive.

A more serious challenge for the traditionalist occurs in 1 Corinthians 11:5 where Paul explicitly mentions women who prophesy in the church. Since women may prophesy, how can there be anything wrong with their teaching or preaching? Or so the argument goes. The traditionalist counters by noting that Paul explicitly separates the roles of prophesying and teaching (Romans 12:6-7, 1 Corinthians 12:28).

While the Bible does not prohibit women from prophesying, Paul does regulate "the demeanor in which they prophesy so as not to compromise the principle of the spiritual leadership of men (1 Corinthians 11:5-10)."[31] Hence, traditionalists insist, "Prophecy in the early church did not correspond to the sermon today or to a formal exposition of Scripture. Both women and men could stand and share what they believed God had brought to mind for the good of the church."[32] But this was not teaching or preaching; and it certainly did not include the work of a pastor or elder.

Even if we are traditionalists or equalitarians, it is easy to see how this debate would be regarded as hopelessly dead-locked. Is there any way to end this stalemate?

FOUR POSITIONS IN THE DEBATE BETWEEN TRADITIONALISTS AND EQUALITARIANS

In an article for the *Journal for the Evangelical Theological Society*, Bruce Barron points out four positions open to participants in the debate between traditionalists and biblical equalitarians.[33]

Dogmatic Equalitarianism	Non-Dogmatic Equalitarianism	Tolerant Traditionalism	Intolerant Traditionalism

People who are *intolerant traditionalists* "reject women in leadership and are *angry* that anyone is suggesting otherwise." Tolerant traditionalists, on the other hand, "reject women in leadership *but* recognize that others may reasonably differ."

Dogmatic equalitarians "believe that women should lead and *dogmatically* enforce their viewpoint by installing women at every level of leadership." Finally, *non-dogmatic equalitarians* believe that women *can* lead, but "recognize the diversity of opinion and do not make acceptance of women in leadership a test of fellowship or an absolute necessity."[34]

Barron's distinctions provide the basis for my conclusion to this chapter. Based on what we've seen of the biblical evidence, the two extreme positions—dogmatic equalitarianism and intolerant traditionalism—are divisive and fail to reflect serious interaction with the complexities and ambiguities of the matter. Traditionalists must learn to be tolerant and recognize that Christians who disagree may have good reasons for doing so. In a similar way, equalitarians should avoid the kind of arrogant dogmatism that so often characterizes supporters of the feminist cause, especially in mainline denominations.

I'm proposing that sincere proponents of equalitarianism and traditionalism manifest the same kind of tolerance we've learned to expect in disagreements over baptism. When we can't persuade others that our understanding of baptism is correct, then mature Christians agree to disagree. This disagreement does not prevent us from cooperating and having fellowship in ways that advance God's Kingdom.

Many Christians will continue to be puzzled over the issue of women leaders in the church. Others will take a position, either on the side of traditionalism or biblical equalitarianism. But surely we can all find ways to disagree that reflect love and tolerance toward those with whom we disagree.

Chapter Three

THE CONTROVERSY OVER RADICAL FEMINISM

❖

T his chapter will explore the relatively new world of radical feminism, especially as it poses numerous threats to the historic Christian faith. As we saw in the last chapter, people within the church do disagree over leadership roles for women. But the kind of feminism that will come into focus in this chapter holds views that I believe all evangelical Christians must reject.

In their revolutionary quest for totally new ways of seeing and thinking about the world and human relationships, radical feminists are not simply at war with men and women who support the traditionalist or biblical equalitarian positions discussed in the last chapter. In their task of constructing a new social order, radical feminists are also waging war against commonsense feminists. In fact, a new term is necessary to distinguish the radical feminists from commonsense feminists—that term is *gender-feminism.*

EVALUATION OF GENDER-FEMINISM

Commonsense feminists believe that discrimination against any person (male or female) on the basis of sex is wrong. Sensible feminists do not deny that there are some relevant differences between the sexes. There seem to be good reasons, for example, to limit the position of middle linebacker on National Football League teams to men. While commonsense feminists want equity with men, they recognize that some differences in roles are justifiable.

The War on Gender Itself

Gender-feminism, however, is a whole different ball game. Radical gender-feminists have not declared war on inequality and discrimination; their battle is with gender itself. Radical or gender-feminism has as its ultimate goal the elimination of all distinctions between the sexes. As American philosopher Christina Hoff Sommers explains,

> [Gender-feminism] is not primarily concerned with more opportunities for women, or, for that matter, with including women's achievements in the [educational] curriculum. Its aim is to transform our understanding of our past, our present and our future. How? By convincing people to accept the central insight of contemporary feminist philosophy: that the sex/gender system is the most important aspect of human relations.[1]

While the average woman, Sommers continues, "has been generally receptive to moderate feminism's claims for greater equality of opportunity, expanded civil and legal rights, and so forth, she is not ready to reject marriage, family and motherhood or the other institutions which the gender feminists tell her she should not want and which will only end up making her another victim."[2]

Gender-feminists, Sommers explains, "share an ideal of a genderless culture that inspires their rejection of such entrenched social arrangements as the family, marriage and maternal responsibilities for child rearing. They also call not only for a radical re-ordering of society but . . . a revolution in knowledge itself, which would extirpate masculine bias, replacing the 'male-centered [college curriculum]' with a new curriculum inspired by a radical feminist perspective."[3]

Other Features of Gender-Feminism

British author William Oddie argues that anger and resentment play a central role in the consciousness of radical feminists. Feeling aggrieved, he declares, "appears to be itself a necessary primary objective [for gender-feminists]. It is a statement of mind, almost a spiritual condition, which seems at times not so much a natural reaction to perceived injustice as itself a means of perception, a kind of lens through which familiar landmarks can take on horrid and undreamed-of-shapes."[4]

Another characteristic of the radical feminist is the belief that she possesses a special way of understanding reality, a power lacking in non-feminist women. Her new feminist consciousness gives her unique types of knowledge that, among other things, make it possible for her and others like her to explain for the first time in history the true relationship between men and women. Such appeals to special avenues of knowledge are strikingly similar to the ancient heresy known as Gnosticism.[5] Like the Gnostics, the radical feminist places her experiences and her understanding of things above God's revelation in the Bible.

A third feature of radical feminism is the resentment its adherents feel toward Christianity, which they reject as patriarchal or male-dominated. This leads them to seek a new religion where powerful female role models take center stage. In these new religions, the cosmos takes on a female nature. This accounts for the radical feminists' turn to one or more varieties of the ancient, pagan goddess religions. As Denise Lardner Carmody explained, "By linking women to a female sacral power, the new Goddess-devotee is affirming herself, saying that what makes God God is as much in her as in men."[6]

The Feminist Move Toward Pantheism and Paganism

While goddess religion plays various roles in the thinking of feminists, it suggests the pantheistic way in which radical feminists see nature and their relationship with nature.[7] "The tendency of Goddess religion," Carmody states, "is to exalt female creativity and cyclicism. The Goddess is the prime symbol of life-bearing, nurturing, waxing and waning. She [the Goddess] says that blood, childbearing, nursing, flowing and ebbing are the quintessence of living Being."[8]

Hence, the destination of radical, anti-Christian feminists is a pagan spirituality, where God is no longer the God of the Bible but the goddess of pre-Christian paganism. Naomi Goldenberg, a Jewish feminist, advocates a restoration of the religion of witchcraft with its emphasis on the cycles of nature. Goldenberg also issues a warning when she states that "there will of course be nothing to prevent people who practice new religions from calling themselves Christians."[9] And they do. In fact, representatives of witchcraft and other forms of paganism are regularly invited guests in the chapels of seminaries belonging to such denominations as the Presbyterian Church USA and the United Methodist Church.

Many radical feminists admit that substituting a goddess-mother for God the Father is equivalent to starting an entirely new religion. Starhawk, a self-described witch, acknowledges that "the symbolism of the Goddess is not a parallel structure to the symbolism of God the Father. The Goddess does not rule the world; she *is* the world. Manifest in each of us, She can be known internally by every individual, in all her magnificent diversity."[10]

It would be unwise to approach the subject of religious feminism while ignoring the deep hurt many women have suffered. Elizabeth Achtemeier of Union Theological Seminary (Richmond, Virginia) maintains, "Feminism has invaded the realm of God, and in some instances, the God of the Christian faith has been replaced with a god or goddess of the feminists' making."[11] However badly representatives of the church have treated women in the past, this is no reason, Achtemeier argues, "to encourage some women to alter the church's basic authority in the Scriptures. The freedom of both females and males rests firmly upon the foundation laid in Jesus Christ and mediated through the Scriptures. If that scriptural foundation is undermined . . . the gospel of freedom will be lost with it. It is not the Bible that is at fault, but the teaching of it."[12]

This background information provides a foundation for our approach to the major question of this chapter: How does radical gender-feminism threaten the historic Christian faith? In the material that follows, I will explore this question with reference to the anti-evangelical (or theologically liberal) feminists.

EVALUATION OF ANTI-EVANGELICAL FEMINISM

I have referred several times to the ease with which theologically liberal feminists abandon essential Christian beliefs. It will be helpful to examine several specific examples of such thinkers and the extent to which they are willing to stretch the meaning of the word *Christian*.

Rejecting Unwanted Portions of the Bible

Rosemary Radford Reuther, a Roman Catholic, teaches theology at Garrett-Evangelical Theological Seminary, a school affiliated with Northwestern University. She uses an attack on biblical authority as the foundation for the rest of her theological system. "Theologically speaking," she writes, "whatever diminishes or denies the full humanity of women must be presumed not to reflect the divine or an authentic relation to the divine."[13] One consequence of this principle is that Reuther rejects any portion of the Bible that she thinks supports patriarchy or otherwise diminishes womanhood.

Somewhat incredibly, some anti-evangelical feminists

think Reuther is too conservative. Their reason for saying this is that she gives the Bible a place in her system of thought. She does this because she thinks the Bible itself supplies the standard by which to recognize the alleged errors in Scripture and hence criticize it. While this principle is found in the Old Testament prophets, Reuther thinks it reaches its most perfect expression in the teaching of Jesus who, she argues, "renews the prophetic vision whereby the Word of God does not validate the existing social and religious hierarchy but speaks on behalf of the marginalized and despised groups of society."[14]

Reuther's test of any feminist theology is the extent to which it advances what she judges to be the full humanity of women. Along with the Bible, she uses such anti-Christian systems as Marxism and pre-Christian pagan traditions. The advancement of feminist objectives plays a far more important role in her theology than does any commitment to any specific biblical or Christian standard. Reuther wants not only a new theology but also a new canon of writings and ideas that will include some of the very pagan beliefs the Bible was written to counter.

The Primal Matrix: Feminism's Pantheism

Reuther's god is "the Primal Matrix, the great womb within which all things, Gods and humans, sky and earth, human and nonhuman beings are generated."[15] She intends none of this language as metaphorical. Reuther's theology obviously rejects divine transcendence in favor of pantheism; it is irreconcilable with anything that is remotely biblical. The distance between her views and those of historic Christianity are apparent in her rejection of conscious, personal survival after death. At death, Reuther believes, our individual selves are reabsorbed back into the cosmic matrix of matter/energy. You and I as conscious individual selves will cease to exist.

Elizabeth Achtemeier points out the contrast between Reuther's hopeless denial of meaning and purpose and the position of historic Christianity. In Achtemeier's words, "The testimony of biblical faith is that the individual does matter—that the Good Shepherd knows his own and his own know him, and that each individual life is held precious . . . within the context of a beloved community that has one flock and one Shepherd (John 10:14-18)."[16] Because goddess religion denies the possibility of conscious, personal existence after death, it cheapens the value of life and makes individual human lives meaningless. While Reuther professes to be a Christian, she is actually an evangelist for the pagan Canaanite religion that is condemned in Scripture.

Some Feminists Believe All the Bible Is Patriarchal

Another anti-evangelical feminist is Elizabeth Schüssler Fiorenza, a professor of New Testament at Harvard Divinity School. Fiorenza ironically regards Reuther as too conservative. Her reason is that Reuther located themes in the Bible that provide a foundation of sorts for her feminist theology. Not so for Fiorenza, who thinks that *all* of the Bible is corrupted by patriarchalism. Fiorenza states that "the locus or place of divine revelation [is] . . . not the Bible or the tradition of a patriarchal church but the *eklesia* [the church or called out ones] of women and the lives of women who live the 'option for our women slaves.'. . . [The place of revelation] is not simply 'the experience' of women but the experience of women . . . struggling for liberation from patriarchal oppression."[17]

For Fiorenza, the canon of truth and revelation must come *not* "from the biblical writings but from the contemporary struggle of women against racism, sexism and poverty as oppressive systems of patriarchy and from its systematic explorations in feminist theory."[18] Only those parts of the Bible that satisfy Fiorenza's criterion, that advance the cause of feminist liberation, are useful.

Further, Jesus plays no normative role in Fiorenza's account of Christian theology. She doubts that anyone can identify anything that counts as an essential Christian belief except, of course, for *her* belief that the liberation of the oppressed is the ultimate norm of all religious "truth."

SOME CRITICISMS OF THE RADICAL RELIGIOUS FEMINISTS

We've already seen that significant criticisms of theologically liberal feminists who claim to represent the Christian faith have come from Elizabeth Achtemeier. Achtemeier is a theologian at the Union Theological Seminary in Richmond, Virginia—a school not known as a conservative or evangelical seminary. As Achtemeier sees it, "There can be no doubt that several feminist theologians are in the process of laying the foundations for a new faith and a new church that are, at best, only loosely related to apostolic Christianity."[19]

Achtemeier has strong sympathy for women seeking justice from fellow Christians. In spite of the clear examples one finds both in Jesus and in the New Testament, she states, the Christian church has too often treated women as second class Christians. "If the church had lived up to its gospel, in which we are all one in Christ Jesus, we would not be in our feminist mess today," she contends.[20] But having said this, Achtemeier objects to the way in which so many feminist extremists have "made their experience the ultimate authority, above the Scriptures. Their liberation has become their all-consuming occupation, coloring everything they write, say and do. The radicals among them have even begun to claim that they have a goddess in themselves, or that they are divine, because they have substituted for the biblical God a 'Primal Matrix' or 'Mother Goddess' or great world spirit flowing in and through all things and people."[21]

In seeking to gain liberation from one type of oppression, they have traded it for a far more serious "captivity to sin and bondage to one's feeble, mortal person."

To make things even worse, many church leaders, she writes, "have almost totally surrendered to such ways of death, perhaps from a sense of guilt over the past treatment of females or from a real sense of justice, but often without thought or theological understanding of the consequences." Because of such actions, "the rest of the church may find its liturgy changed by some worship committee into a celebration of a Canaanite, fertility birthing god, or it may discover that it is no longer allowed to sing a hymn based on Isaiah 63."

All the while, these feminists lecture other Christians on the suspicious nature of the Scriptures, which should be accepted as true only when they conform to modern feminist teaching.

The Construction of the "Women-Church"
"Alongside the body of Christ," Achtemeier continues, "some feminists are constructing a new church, called women-church, and celebrating a new religion, sometimes utilizing the symbol of a female 'Christa' on a cross." It is difficult to imagine any more confining bondage to one's sinful self and society. Repeated study of extreme feminism within the church brought Achtemeier to a new realization that "the only freedom from one's sinful self lies in that liberty given us by Christ."

The Criticism of the Call for Inclusive Language
Achtemeier has recently directed her criticism of anti-evangelical feminists to their call for the use of inclusive language in all references to God. When male terms are used of God, radical feminists argue, the language can too easily be taken literally and thus encourage situations that perpetuate male domination over women. This must be avoided, they insist, by referring to God as "She." In American seminaries, some of them supposedly evangelical, professors and students pray publicly to "God our Mother." Extreme feminists frequently replace what they regard as male-oriented titles like "Lord," "King," and "Son of

God," for neutral terms like "Sovereign," "Ruler," and "Child of God." In still other attempts to remove any male connotations to names of God, one can find them referring to God with words like "Wisdom," "Holy One," or "Defender."

An example of inclusive language in action appears in the book *WomanSpirit Rising*, where the following prayer for Jewish women is commended:

> Blessed is She who Spoke and the world became.
>   Blessed is She.
> Blessed is She who in the beginning, gave birth. . . .
> Blessed is She whose womb covers the earth.
> Blessed is She whose womb protects all creatures.[22]

Feminists Changing the Concept of God

Feminist extremists are not content with inclusive language in references to God. They are busy changing the very concept of God. Rita Gross describes God as a "bisexual androgynous deity."[23] In the words of Starhawk,

> There is no dichotomy between spirit and flesh, no split between Godhead and the world. The Goddess is manifest in the world; she brings life into being, is Nature, is flesh. . . . The Goddess is also earth—Mother Earth, who sustains all growing things, who is the body, our bones and cells. . . . She is found in the world around us, in the cycles and seasons of nature, and in mind, body, spirit, and all the emotions within each of us. Thou art Goddess. I am Goddess. All that lives (and all that is, lives), all that serves life, is Goddess.[24]

Starhawk's paragraph is a crude version of a feminist, pagan pantheism. It would be difficult to imagine anything more removed from the worldview of Judaism and Christianity. Yet this anti-Christian paganism is even embraced by feminists who claim to represent evangelicalism. Virginia Mollenkott now speaks of God as giving birth to the universe.[25]

When female terminology and images are used of God, it becomes impossible to avoid the image of giving birth. And so, Achtemeier warns, "If a female deity gives birth to the universe . . . it follows that all things participate in the life or in the substance and divinity of that deity—in short, that *the creator is indissolubly bound up with the creation*. And this is exactly what one finds in feminist theologies."[26] In this way, the crude pantheism of the anti-Christian feminists like Starhawk finds a home in feminists like Reuther and Mollenkott who claim to be Christians, in some greatly extended sense of the word. In fact, Achtemeier finds the presuppositions of Mollenkott to be "little different from those of Starhawk, who writes out of the pagan context of modern witchcraft's covens."[27]

THE GODDESS MOVEMENT
IN MAINLINE DENOMINATIONS

It hardly seems coincidental that a number of liberal seminaries in the U.S. have provided platforms for the witch Starhawk and other anti-Christian feminists. Starhawk has spoken at San Francisco Theological Seminary, an institution affiliated with the Presbyterian Church USA. A similar episode involving the Perkins School of Theology, a seminary affiliated with Southern Methodist University in Dallas, was reported by *National and International Religion Report*. According to the publication, "Methodist seminary officials in Dallas [at Perkins] found themselves in a caldron after a witch was invited to lecture and lead a liturgy to an ancient deity."

As the report described the event, "Linda Finnell, a self-avowed occultist and lesbian, gave her presentation during a 'Women's Week' series sponsored by Perkins School of Theology. . . . The special class was held at posh Highland Park United Methodist Church in Dallas. One observer said that Finnell 'projected a positive affirmation of witchcraft' while she lectured behind a candlelit altar featuring an image of the goddess Diana."[28]

In a related item, the same publication quoted a leader of the "Good News Movement" in the United Methodist Church to the effect that "controversy is brewing over the issue of goddess worship in mainline denominations."[29] According to James Heidinger of Good News,

> A strong feminist bent among some seminarians has led to the adoption of non-traditional references to God, such as "Mother God" or "Mother-Father God," thus encouraging a search for a goddess figure in the scriptures. Although he does not believe the trend is finding favor in the pews, Heidinger said reports indicate such ideas are being disseminated widely in theological schools. "There are some [Methodist] seminaries where you can't even refer to God as Father," Heidinger claimed. One female seminarian at Perkins reportedly closes prayers in the name of the female goddess, he added.[30]

Achtemeier's objections to radical feminist theology have hardly begun. She points out that a number of feminist theologians no longer believe God is needed. Moreover, "because feminist theology understands human beings to participate in or incarnate the divine within themselves, there is little realistic understanding of the nature of human sin."[31] Feminist extremists echo radical-liberation theologians who "maintain that they can, by their own power, restructure society, restore creation, and overcome suffering."[32] Their refusal to recognize the truth of the biblical teaching about sin leads them inevitably to utopian ways of thinking.

Misrepresentation of God's Nature
As serious as all these other errors are, they still place second to the feminist's misrepresentation of the nature of God. And so

Achtemeier examines the pantheism that follows the feminists' failure to distinguish God from His creation. This kind of error becomes inevitable, Achtemeier explains, "when the feminists reject any notion of the inspiration of the [Bible], make their own experience their authority, and use female language for God. As soon as God is called female, the images of birth, of suckling, of carrying in the womb, and most importantly, the identification of the deity with the life in all things become inevitable, and the Bible's careful and consistent distinction between Creator and creation is blurred and lost."[33]

Inclusive language in references to God is hardly a benign issue, then. The Christian church must not surrender to faddish demands to refer to God in feminine terms. Whenever the church does this, either by rewriting hymns, in prayers, or by feminist translations of Scripture, it begins traveling down the road to a new concept of deity.

The radical feminists who insist on regarding themselves as "Christians" have moved far beyond the kinds of theological liberalism perpetrated by their male predecessors. They are moving in the direction of a goddess religion that is the very antithesis of historic Judaism and biblical Christianity.

Donald Bloesch, professor of theology at Dubuque School of Theology, points to another irony in the feminist move toward a goddess religion: "Women were able to gain a real place of stature in Hebraic religion, even though the patriarchal culture was still intact. On the other hand, women were often held in low esteem in the cultures dominated by the fertility cults."[34] While the major symbol in Babylonian goddess religion was female, Bloesch observes, *that religion reduced women to sex objects*. Efforts to revive such a religion is an odd attempt to honor women or elevate their status.

Bloesch urges feminists to remember "that the chief threat to biblical faith was in the goddess religion of the fertility cults of the ancient Near East."[35] The prophets of the Old Testament, however, "were adamant that there could be no synthesis with this type of religion but only exclusion and replacement. Their stance was based not on a commitment to patriarchy . . . but on a steadfast resolve to remain true to the basic vision of their faith that God revealed himself as sovereign Lord, as *one* and as the *only* God."[36]

THE AUTHOR'S VIEW

Donald Bloesch and Elizabeth Achtemeier, along with a relatively small number of others who vocally oppose the new (or old) pagan religion of the radical feminists, deserve the thanks of evangelicals. The language we use to refer to God does make a difference.

But the leadership they have demonstrated in this matter makes one wonder about the large number of self-described evangelical feminists who ignore the serious theological inadequacies of the more radical feminists. Some evangelical feminists support the use of inclusive language in references to God. Their silence about the theological excesses of feminist extremists creates the impression that some regard the feminism issue as more important than biblical authority and doctrinal integrity. The evangelical feminists seem to be saying that since the radicals support us on this one important cause (feminism), we'll give them a free ride on other issues. When these other issues include heresy, I don't think there should be a free ride.

Evangelical feminists, whose thought and ethic is supposedly under the control of Scripture, should be criticizing the feminist extremists. We have noticed a few voices raised in protest, but the truth is that most evangelical feminists have remained silent in the face of gender-feminism's most egregious faults. I believe, by their silence, that evangelical feminists are aiding the spread within the church of a movement that denies the biblical understanding of the very nature of God.

CONCLUSION

The purpose of this chapter has been to draw attention to some major features of contemporary, radical feminism. Further, I've tried to show the variety of views on the subject. I've argued for biblical lines to be drawn and for self-described evangelical feminists to consider allowing their views to be reformed by biblical thinking.

As William Oddie warned, "There are wide open lines of communication between feminists within the church and post-Christian feminists decidedly outside it, with few discernible doctrinal inhibitions or overriding biblical loyalties to anchor Christian feminists clearly within their own tradition."[37] While it might appear that Oddie is referring primarily to theologically liberal feminists and not evangelical feminists, I don't think we can let evangelical feminists off the hook this easily. For one thing, we have the example of Virginia Mollenkott to consider. As a second example, we have a 1990 book titled *Gender Matters* in which a dozen or so faculty members at a well-known evangelical college illustrate how some evangelical feminists have joined the more radical feminist parade.[38]

In a noteworthy review-essay about *Gender Matters*, Terri Graves Taylor argues that much more is at stake in discussions of gender than simply the equal treatment of women. Feminists these days have an agenda that is much different from the purpose of the church. And evangelicals who join the feminist line ought to be asking where the line is leading.

Taylor applauds the intention of the contributors to *Gender Matters* to fill in gaps by discussing previously ignored or forgotten women in fields like politics and the letters. However, she is troubled by the failure of the writers "to critically engage feminism, to explore fully what changes the feminists are asking of us."[39] What will happen, she asks, when evangelicals fall into line and buy the radical feminist claim that *all* knowledge is ideologically controlled? Such a position would deprive us of any fixed point from which we could possibly judge and evaluate any other position. Feminists seem oblivious to the fact that such a position would eliminate any ground for attacking patriarchy. It would also deprive us of any ground on which to defend Christianity.

If all knowledge *is* ideologically controlled, then radical feminists have no rational ground for their position; indeed, this viewpoint would make the attainment of a rational position on any subject impossible. Yet Christian faith *rests* on historical, rational events and rational propositions in the Bible. Evangelical feminists should not allow their desire to promote just treatment of women to blind them to the serious threats to Christianity that are an unavoidable feature of radical feminism.

Chapter Four

THE CONTROVERSY OVER
DIVORCE AND REMARRIAGE

F ew events in life produce a wider range of intense emotions than a wedding. The new husband and wife, their
parents, families, and friends, and their church share a
common set of hopes and dreams for the new family. The tragic
death of those dreams along with the bitterness, alienation, and
hatred that so often mark the end of a marriage make divorce a
spiritual as well as a moral disaster.

The days when Christians could view divorce as a problem
for people outside the church ceased to exist long ago. These
days, the number of single-parent families within churches
is growing at a rate two-and-a-half times that of two-parent
families. The number of failed marriages within evangelical
churches is fast approaching a crisis mark.

In spite of this, many pastors are doing little or nothing to
help strengthen troubled marriages. Even less is done to minister to the hurting spouses and children after divorce or to
counsel divorced people who are considering remarriage. Many
evangelicals have never heard sermons that offered a biblical
perspective on divorce and remarriage.

This is not to say there are *no* efforts being made to

minister to the newly divorced single adults in this country. A great number of large innovative churches have more than one staff member involved in ministry to singles and single-parent families.[1] There are more and more divorce recovery workshops for both parents and children and innovative ministries to divorced parents.

The problem is, too many congregations and senior pastors fail to realize the scope of the divorce epidemic in this country. One out of two marriages end in divorce. This means that ministry to those who have been divorced is as much a part of the church as ministry to the nuclear family! Further, there are now many blended families (where two divorced people get remarried and combine their children). Hardly any extended family—much less any whole congregation—is untouched by divorce.

The emergence of divorce and remarriage as a problem within conservative churches is leading many pastors and parishioners to choose sides. On the one hand, Craig Blomberg explains, "More and more believers are reacting against the crumbling morality of contemporary society with the imposition of tight and absolute prohibitions [regarding divorce and remarriage]."[2] If the leaders of such a church cannot find a biblical text that justifies divorce or remarriage in a specific case, the church simply forbids the action. Couples who divorce and/or remarry contrary to the ruling of the church leaders realize the necessity of leaving that fellowship.

Some churches are dealing with these issues in a rigid way. But as Blomberg explains, "Increasing numbers of Christians in quite different circles have virtually resigned themselves to expect and accept fellow believers being divorced on all kinds of less serious grounds. Such people would scarcely dream of ever confronting their friends and saying, 'You are wrong, you are sinning against God and your family, and you need to repent!' "[3]

It can often be difficult for the governing leadership of churches to insist on biblical standards on divorce and remarriage in an age in which so many people think that anything is permitted. It is a matter of great urgency that Christians think through what Scripture teaches and formulate principles to guide their thinking and conduct on these matters. After a pastor has formulated his understanding of the biblical principles that apply, he should share them with the church on a regular basis. His sermons should provide help for troubled marriages. He should carefully explain the situations within which he will marry divorced people.

The many positions people take with regard to divorce can be reduced to the following four options:

A	B	C	D
Divorce is never permissible, whatever the reason.	Divorce is permissible in a limited number of extreme cases.	Divorce is permissible in many cases; some reasons, however, do not justify divorce.	Divorce is permissible for any reason whatsoever.

The *D* position, that divorce is permissible for any reason, used to be confined pretty much to nonChristians. Openness to the *D* position on the part of any church or denomination is probably a sign of other serious problems (such as questioning the authority of Scripture or the serious nature of human sin). Believers within those fellowships ought to be concerned to deal with those problems.

Marriages are worth preserving from a number of standpoints. Spiritually, they are covenants between the husband and wife and God. Functionally, they are the foundation of society, and as a number of anthropologists have found, cultures that view marriage as dispensable just don't survive.

Position *A*, that divorce is never permissible, has been a minority position among Christians for a long time.[4] In a 1980 poll taken by *Christianity Today* magazine, only 10 percent of American clergy aligned themselves with this view. A similar percentage of the general public also regarded *A* as their view.[5]

Obviously, a belief may be true even if it is unpopular. Of course, a lot has happened to change American thinking since 1980.

Partly to save time, the rest of this chapter will focus on position *B*, that the Bible permits divorce only in extreme circumstances. As we'll see, the *A* position does appear to conflict with two well-known New Testament texts; hence, it seems too strict. Positions *C* and *D* must be viewed as too loose for Christians who want their thinking to conform to Scripture.

What I have called the *B* position, the belief that divorce is permissible only in extreme circumstances, is actually held in three forms, which I diagram as follows:[6]

The B Position
Divorce is permissible only in extreme circumstances.

B1: There is only one circumstance: adultery.	B2: There are two extreme circumstances: adultery and desertion.	B3: There are a relatively small number of extreme circumstances.

Position B1—divorce is justifiable only when the spouse has committed adultery—is based on a literal reading of Jesus' words in Matthew 5:31-32: "It has been said, 'Anyone who divorces his wife must give her a certificate of divorce.' But I tell you that anyone who divorces his wife, except for marital unfaithfulness, causes her to become an adulteress, and anyone who marries the divorced woman commits adultery."

Position B2—two and only two extreme circumstances justify divorce—is based on Matthew 5:31-32 *plus* Paul's words in 1 Corinthians 7:15, which many understand to say that divorce is justified in cases of desertion: "If the unbeliever leaves, let him do so. A believing man or woman is not bound in such circumstances; God has called us to live in peace." It is interesting to note that position B2 became the major view among theologically conservative Protestants after the Reformation.[7]

Many biblically faithful Christians are convinced, however, that the two identified exceptions are insufficient to cover the agonizingly complex problems of men and women in their churches. Hence, such people have attempted to justify a small, limited number of other circumstances that clearly provide warrant for divorce. Theologian Samuel Mikolaski offers as examples such debilitating evils as "philandering, alcoholism, violence, cruelty, psychotic or serious neurotic conditions, homosexuality, impotence, sociopathic behavior, abandonment, extended imprisonment, incest, and abortion without consent of the husband." Mikolaski argues, "There is no warrant in Scripture to submit to such evils. In some cases spiritual heroism on the part of a suffering spouse may be redemptive. Where redemptive steps prove fruitless, most Christians understand the Scriptures to allow merciful escape from such evils."[8]

I know advocates of positions B1 and B2 who maintain, for example, that a Christian wife has no right to a divorce even if a deranged husband threatens her life or abuses the children or engages in any similar act. Such an attitude, some have suggested, displays an insensitivity to the threatened or injured parties that is inconsistent with biblical values.

The problem is, of course, that the Bible does seem to limit divorce to cases of sexual immorality alone (on one interpretation) or to the additional ground of desertion. Clearly, some have said, there is need to examine the biblical grounds for divorce more thoroughly. In the pursuit of that objective, the rest of this chapter will explore a biblically faithful answer to the following questions:

What is the biblical view of marriage?
What does God think of divorce?
Are there any scriptural grounds for divorce? If so, what are they?
Can a biblical case be made for divorce in extreme circumstances other than sexual immorality and desertion?
What about the remarriage of divorced persons?

The necessary starting point for any reflection about divorce should be a proper biblical understanding of marriage. We can hardly expect couples who marry without comprehending what marriage should be to see why divorce is portrayed as it is in Scripture.

THE BIBLICAL VIEW OF MARRIAGE

Many people, perhaps the majority of people in our society, hold a view of marriage that can best be described as utilitarian or pragmatic. Something has value for a utilitarian if it produces desirable consequences. Something is good for a pragmatist if it works. For people who view marriage in this way, the question of when a marriage should be ended is simple—when it no longer gives the husband or wife what he or she wants from the marriage. When the marriage no longer produces the desired consequences or when one partner believes his or her needs can be better met under different circumstances, thoughts turn toward the most convenient ways of breaking the union. Some find shedding a spouse no different from trading in an old car for a newer one. If you happen to see something you like better, find a way to dump the old partner.

While this picture may be a bit crude and certainly does not describe all divorces, it is hardly credible to deny that this way of thinking exists or that many churches look the other way when this sort of thing happens. Too many Americans resist the suggestion that divorce is *wrong*, that it is caused by sin, that it is displeasing to God, and that the church may find it necessary to discipline people who knowingly violate God's moral demands. One reason, then, why Western society tolerates such a high incidence of divorce is because so many people hold a shallow, utilitarian, unbiblical view of marriage.

In contrast to the utilitarian view of marriage, theologian Samuel Mikolaski explains that in the Bible, marriage "is a gift of God in creation to the human race and that monogamous marriage, as a bond between two covenanting persons, is intended to be permanent (Genesis 2:24)." Mikolaski also points out that the Bible does not talk about marriage in any abstract sense, but presents it rather "as a unique kind of personal relationship involving deep, loving commitment to each other."[9]

The ideas of *covenant* and *permanence* are central in the biblical view of marriage. A covenant, D. J. Atkinson explains, "is a personal relationship within a publicly known structure, based on promises given and accepted."[10] The Bible elevates marriage to the highest possible human level by comparing it to the covenants God makes with human beings. The relationship between Jesus Christ and His church is offered as the model of human relationships within marriage. Husbands are to love their wives as Christ loved the church and gave His life for her (Ephesians 5:25). Wives are to submit to their husbands as the church submits to Christ. A covenantal relationship that fits this biblical pattern, a relationship pursued by two Spirit-filled believers living in accordance with God's revealed Word, would seem to be in little danger from the scourge of divorce.

Once the biblical view of marriage is understood, it becomes clear that God's ideal regarding marriage is permanence. "Haven't you read," Jesus taught, "that at the beginning the Creator 'made them male and female,' and said, 'For this reason a man will leave his father and mother and be united to his wife, and the two will become one flesh'? So they are no longer two, but one. Therefore what God has joined together, let man not separate" (Matthew 19:4-6).

WHAT DOES GOD THINK OF DIVORCE?

When people have a more profound view of marriage, they will be less likely to hold a casual view of divorce. Divorce is clearly serious business; it reflects the fact that sin has broken what should have been an inviolable covenant. It is no wonder then that the prophet Malachi stated, "'I hate divorce,' says the LORD

God of Israel" (2:16). Those who believe that divorce is permissible for any whim or inclination suffer from an unbiblical understanding of marriage, or from a questionable understanding of God's Word, or else from a dangerous misunderstanding of how seriously our Holy God takes such matters.

ARE THERE ANY SCRIPTURAL GROUNDS FOR DIVORCE?

The key Old Testament text on divorce is Deuteronomy 24:1-4, which reads:

> If a man marries a woman who becomes displeasing to him because he finds something indecent about her, and he writes her a certificate of divorce, gives it to her and sends her from his house, and if after she leaves his house she becomes the wife of another man, and her second husband dislikes her and writes her a certificate of divorce, gives it to her and sends her from his house, or if he dies, then her first husband, who divorced her, is not allowed to marry her again after she has been defiled. That would be detestable in the eyes of the LORD.

It is a mistake to regard these words as an expression of God's approval of divorce. Rather, as D. J. Atkinson points out, this Old Testament legislation "affords recognition of the fact that marriages are sometimes broken, although divorce is not approved; it acknowledges the need of civil legislation for the sake of society (bill of divorcement); it serves to protect the divorced woman and to legislate against cruelty. In its own negative way, therefore, it is seeking to preserve the divine ideal for marriage as far as possible within a sinful world."[11] In other words, the real purpose of the legislation was to control the practice of divorce and to protect the wife.

As for the New Testament, the debate over the biblical grounds for divorce centers around two passages. The first is Matthew 19:8-9—"Moses permitted you to divorce your wives because your hearts were hard. But it was not this way from the beginning. I tell you that anyone who divorces his wife, except for marital unfaithfulness [Greek: *porneia*], and marries another woman commits adultery." With few exceptions, commentators agree that *porneia* justifies divorce. Under no circumstances, however, does Jesus command the wronged party to seek divorce; He simply states that it is permitted.

The second text is 1 Corinthians 7:15, which refers to an unbelieving spouse leaving the believer. Paul says in effect, "Let the deserting spouse go!" He then adds that in such circumstances, the believer is no longer bound, which most commentators understand to mean that the deserted spouse is free to divorce.

That's it. That is all the New Testament says to provide explicit grounds for divorce. Of course, that is not all that Christian commentators on this issue have had to say. I will now turn my attention to what *porneia* and desertion mean. In particular, I will be seeking an answer to this question: Are *porneia* and desertion the *only* extreme circumstances under which Christians are permitted to seek divorce?

What Is *Porneia*?

Jesus clearly permitted divorce in cases where a spouse is guilty of *porneia*. It is commonly thought that Jesus was referring exclusively to adultery. That seems unlikely, however. Had that been Jesus' point, He could have used a different Greek word, *moicheia*, the usual word for cases of adultery. It seems more reasonable to conclude "that *porneia* is a term that refers to sexual immorality in general, and that within this general classification it may refer to a number of specified sins, depending on its context."[12]

It might help at this point to picture a large circle and

then a number of smaller circles all contained within the bigger one. What Jesus called *porneia* is indicated by the bigger circle. We can label the larger circle *sexual immorality* in general. The smaller circles then would stand for specific types of sexual immorality, such as prostitution, incest, homosexuality, unchastity, adultery, and so on.

If this line of thinking is correct, the grounds for divorce in Matthew 19:9 includes forms of sexual immorality other than adultery. It could most certainly include homosexuality and sexual abuse.

But now something very interesting arises. The same word (*porneia*) is used to refer to *spiritual* unfaithfulness or betrayal. In Hosea 1:2, God speaks of the spiritual betrayal by Israel as *porneia*. The same point is made repeatedly in Jeremiah 3.[13] In a later section of this chapter, I'll consider the suggestion of some that this new usage of *porneia* opens the possibility of some interesting new dimensions to Jesus' teaching in Matthew 19:9.

What Is Desertion?
Paul is very blunt in 1 Corinthians 7:15. If an unbelieving spouse deserts a believer, let him go! The marriage is over. Not only is the deserted believer under no obligation to try to stop the divorce, the believer is free to remarry. This is the clear implication of Paul's words.

This text can be approached in a few different ways.

1. Some people see the text as providing an additional ground for divorce besides the sexual immorality covered in Matthew 19:9. A small number of these people think this proves that Jesus' words in Matthew 19:9 were never intended as an exhaustive list of the grounds for divorce.

2. Others maintain that since *porneia* carries the broader meaning of spiritual betrayal, the desertion mentioned in 1 Corinthians 7:15 may be viewed as an instance of *porneia*, understood in this broader sense. On this reading, desertion

is not a second or new ground for divorce. It is rather one of several instances of the one basic ground, *porneia*. Understood in this way, it becomes reasonable to regard such acts as physical abuse, attempted murder, extreme physical or mental cruelty, and similar serious violations of the marriage covenant as biblically justifiable grounds for divorce.

3. Still others disagree with the two previous views. They agree that *porneia* may refer to forms of sexual immorality other than adultery. But whatever the full extent of *porneia* may be, they insist that it must be limited to acts that break the one-flesh union between husband and wife. People who fall into this third group think it is a mistake to open the meaning of *porneia* up to include spiritual unfaithfulness.

Christian leaders must be ready with a biblical answer for the battered or abused spouse who sincerely wants to know what her Christian duty is regarding her marriage. While recognizing that others disagree, some Christians nonetheless believe they are on solid biblical, theological, and moral ground in advising such a person that she has a right to seek a divorce. It makes good sense, these believers think, to see a spouse who practices physical and/or sexual abuse as someone who has broken the marriage covenant and in a very real sense deserted his spouse. In the extended sense of *porneia* noted above, it becomes more plausible to see that behavior as an act of spiritual betrayal and unfaithfulness. There are other ways to break the marriage covenant than simply by having sex with another person.

In a recent article published in *Trinity Journal*, Craig Blomberg, a New Testament professor at Denver Seminary, takes a closer look at the relation between the sexual immorality of Matthew 19 and the desertion of 1 Corinthians 7. He invites his readers to consider what sexual immorality and desertion have in common. He writes,

> Once one recalls that the marriage covenant contained two main components—personal allegiance or loyalty

and interpersonal intimacy culminating in sexual relations—the answer emerges with surprising ease. Both
infidelity and desertion break one half of the marriage
covenant. Unfaithfulness destroys sexual exclusivity;
desertion reneges on the commitment to "leave and
cleave."[14]

This, he suggests, is why either act justifies divorce: each of
them violates an essential part of the marital covenant. But then,
he asks, why is remarriage permissible (even though not man-
datory) in each case? "Apparently because the very constitu-
ent elements of marriage have been so ruptured that divorce
does not necessarily produce any greater evil, and at times may
actually *prevent* a greater evil."[15]

If there were any real hope of reconciliation, the greater
good of that reunion would rule out divorce, Blomberg suggests. But when a relationship has been destroyed—a natural
consequence of acts as serious as the ones being considered—divorce is probably unavoidable.

Blomberg summarizes his overall view of divorce and
remarriage by saying that God "intends all marriages to be
permanent but gives people the freedom to follow or reject
his intentions. He permits divorce for adultery and desertion
because these sins so undermine the foundation of a marriage
that greater pain or evil may result if legal dissolution does not
occur. Neither of these sins, however, uniquely destroys a marriage; restoration always remains the ideal."[16] Every effort to
reconcile should be made before the marriage is ended. Equally
important, there should be agreement in all this from a supportive Christian community to which the person belongs.

Blomberg's admittedly controversial approach finds wider
ramifications in the Matthew 19 and 1 Corinthians 7 texts
than some Christians are willing to accept. He believes these
passages leave "the door open for divorce as a last resort in
certain other situations where it may also be the lesser of

evils." But even under this somewhat extended set of conditions, he adds, "Divorce should never be considered unless
all other approaches to healing a broken relationship have been
exhausted."[17]

Even for those who agree with Blomberg, there is obvious need for a warning at this point. He repeats his insistence
that divorce is morally permissible under the kinds of conditions he described *as a last resort*. These words are crucial. As
Blomberg explains, "Once one moves beyond clearly definable
grounds for divorce and remarriage, one opens the door to all
kinds of possible abuse of biblical principles."[18] Fallen human
beings will usually think they've reached their last resort long
before they actually have. This would be an appropriate time
for a helpful and supportive community of believers to exercise
an influence.

The same situation occurs for those who restrict the
grounds of divorce to acts that are subclasses of sexual immorality and desertion, as understood in the broad sense. As one
recent denominational report explains,

> The list of sins tantamount to desertion cannot be very
> long. To qualify, a sin must have the same extreme
> effect as someone's physical abandonment of his
> spouse. We are not unaware of the danger which lurks
> behind such a position in the temptation it may pose to
> some to spin out a vast array of marital sins equivalent
> to desertion. This danger, however, we conclude is best
> met in other ways than by an effort to forge a barrier to
> divorce sturdier than the Bible's own.[19]

As we've seen, then, Christians who believe that divorce
is permissible only in extreme circumstances disagree over
whether there is only one extreme circumstance (adultery),
or two extreme circumstances (adultery, desertion), or a relatively small number of extreme circumstances (unfaithfulness,

a broken marriage covenant, spiritual betrayal). Some who take this third position (B3 on our diagram) insist that whatever these other circumstances are, they must be classified under the kind of broad understanding of sexual immorality and desertion explained above. Others take things a bit further and place their emphasis upon words like "as a last resort."

However desirable it would be for the Christians who disagree in these ways to reach agreement, that does not seem likely. Christians who differ in these ways should seek to understand the reasons that people hold a different viewpoint in their search for a biblical and compassionate position.

WHAT ABOUT THE REMARRIAGE OF DIVORCED PERSONS?

Blomberg argues that "divorce in biblical times virtually always carried with it the right to remarry; no [New Testament] text rescinds this permission. Neither partner of a divorced couple, in which both have remained celibate, should consider marrying a new spouse unless serious and sustained attempts to reconciliation (either before or after the divorce) have proved fruitless. Those who are already remarried (or sexually involved) should earnestly repent of any unconfessed sin and commit themselves to faithfulness to making their present marriage honor Christ."[20]

Blomberg's assumption that the right to remarry is presupposed in the New Testament discussion of divorce is contested by many. He is certainly correct that the right to remarry was taken for granted in Jewish culture. The issue is whether this condition in that culture was presupposed by Jesus and Paul. Those on both sides might find it easier to be tolerant of those with whom they disagree if they recognize that any conclusion involves some extrapolation from the specific statements in Scripture.

Whatever conclusion we reach about the broader issue of remarriage, it seems clear that, according to Matthew 19:9 and

1 Corinthians 7:15, the wronged spouse has the right to remarry. It should be noted, however, that in 1 Corinthians 7:15 Paul describes specific situations where the deserting spouse is an unbeliever. This has led some to conclude that in cases when two believers divorce, they are not to remarry (1 Corinthians 7:10-11).

How should churches deal with people who have already remarried following an unbiblical divorce? There is great wisdom in the words of a 1991 report to the General Assembly of the Presbyterian Church in America:

> The gentle use of pastoral oversight will ask parties to seek God's gracious forgiveness by repenting of their past sins in marriage and by rededicating their lives to Christ in the confidence of His forgiveness and His acceptance of their present marriage. That assumes, of course, genuine repentance on their part. We must remember that adultery and divorce are not the unforgivable sin, but that they along with other ungodly sins are covered by the blood of Christ.[21]

WHAT IS THE RESPONSIBILITY OF CHURCH LEADERS?

I began this chapter by noting that many Christian leaders fail in their duty to the children and adults in their congregations who are suffering the consequences of a troubled or broken marriage. Fortunately, large numbers of churches have begun to recognize the responsibility they have to minister to troubled families, to divorced people, to single parents, and to the children of broken homes. There is also a growing awareness of the urgency of helping young people in high school and college to understand the biblical model of marriage.

Our churches should be doing more premarital counseling, which among other things, should discourage couples from marrying too quickly. Our churches also need to teach people about the value of the single life. It is obviously God's will that some people not marry. Churches need to do a better job of ministering to singles and helping them with the special problems they encounter.

Let me urge every pastor reading this chapter to begin preparing at least one message in which he lovingly explains to his congregation his understanding of God's will in marriage, as well as what constitutes the small number of extreme circumstances in which divorce is justified. He should also make public the principles he'll utilize when he responds to divorced people who come to him with remarriage in mind. Every Christian leader should see the urgency of developing counseling skills in these areas. Every church should reexamine what it is doing to minister to individuals threatened by divorce or suffering the consequences of broken marriages.

Divorce is seldom the end of one's problems. The often traumatic breaking of a marriage covenant is followed by many new, often unanticipated difficulties. Church leaders and compassionate church members are presented with an unparalleled opportunity to befriend, help, and minister to people in need.

Chapter Five

THE CONTROVERSY OVER PSYCHOLOGY AND COUNSELING

C indy had just emerged from her therapist's office, feeling more discouraged than ever. On the short walk to her car at the office tech center, across the busy boulevard from the church, she unavoidably ran into the Rev. Jones. Ralph Jones was a dedicated servant of God, an honors graduate from a distinguished evangelical seminary, and the product of an upbringing in a Christian home.

Cindy was nervous as he approached because she knew her former pastor disapproved of her seeking counseling outside the church. That had been the main reason she had left First Church, although she'd never made a formal announcement of that fact. It had only been a few months since she'd sought fellowship at another smaller church on the outskirts of town. Nevertheless, her church attendance had waned from the year before when she and her pastor had had a strained conversation regarding a very difficult counseling situation. She felt ostracized by the whole church, since her "secret" had come out.

As he approached, Cindy decided to make the best of the situation and put on a smile. Pastor Jones greeted her warmly, "Cindy, it's *good* to see you! Been visiting with Dan I see."

"Er, um, yeah, I have, Ralph," Cindy was surprised at his cordial manner. "It was a helpful session; painful, but I think I'm making progress." Ralph frowned and shook his head.

Uh, oh, here it comes, Cindy thought, *another lecture on the evils of psychology.*

But the frown yielded to a look of tenderness and Cindy's puzzled expression in response made Ralph laugh softly. "You know, Cindy, I owe you an apology."

"What?" Cindy gasped, more puzzled than ever.

"You know where I'm headed right now?" he asked her.

"No sir, unless it's in there to give Dan a hard time again," Cindy responded.

Ralph shook his head again, this time with compassion and understanding.

"No ma'am. I am going to see Dan, but it's for me, for Dan's help on my own very real needs."

Cindy was amazed. She could tell Ralph was both serious and repentant over something, but she wasn't sure what. "Tell me more, pastor."

"Well, Cindy," Ralph responded, "it's a long story that Megan [the Reverend's wife] and I should tell you sometime. How about over dinner? Why don't you meet us tonight at that Mexican food place over on North Boulevard? We'll fill you in then. For now, let me just say that I was out of touch when I berated you over your counseling needs last year. I hope that's not why you've been absent from church so much lately."

Cindy turned a bit red.

"Anyway," Ralph continued, "that's something else we can talk about. What's important is that you understand I was foolish in my reaction to your going to Dan for counsel. He's a good man. And frankly, he's ministered to Megan and me more the last few months than anyone since my seminary days. Cindy, he's helped me wake up to so much; I can't wait to tell you the rest."

The smile on Cindy's face was real now. And she felt warmth from the pastor's honesty and apology. She could tell something was going on and it was good.

"Okay, Ralph. Tonight will you tell me the whole story? And maybe I'll be able to talk about why I haven't been at First Church much lately!" She accepted the brief hug from the Reverend, feeling a genuine love restored for this man who had helped her so much in her early Christian experience. Though that seemed far away now, she felt a renewed sense of compassion and excitement. She looked forward to the evening with a sense of anticipation she had not felt in months.

THE SOURCE OF MUCH CONTROVERSY

The Rev. Ralph Jones had been concerned initially over Cindy's seeking Dan's counsel because of a deep distrust of psychology. Dan and Ralph were peers in many ways: Ralph was only a couple of years older than Dan, both were professionals, each had more than one graduate degree, both were highly respected members of the community. Dan had been a model member of First Church, having grown up there before Ralph arrived. Dan had returned from his doctoral work at a respected West Coast Christian university to set up a counseling ministry near the church.

At first Dan had eagerly sought the church's cooperation as he established his ministry. But as things progressed he felt more and more tension between his goals and those of the church leadership, including Ralph. The primary bone of contention was Dan's use of what the elders considered psychological counseling techniques. They were not opposed to *all* counseling. In fact, when they hired Ralph they had specifically requested that he be competent in pastoral counseling.

The Bible Calls for Godly Counsel
The Bible, after all, indicates that godly counsel is important—most notably in the book of Proverbs. It begins with the admonition to seek wisdom, and in the first chapter, gaining wisdom is tied directly to wise and godly counsel: "A wise man

will hear and increase in learning, and a man of understanding will acquire wise counsel" (Proverbs 1:5, NASB). And again in 11:14 (NASB), "Where there is no guidance, the people fall, but in abundance of counselors there is victory."

So it was not counseling as such that concerned Ralph and the elders (and others in the congregation, judging from their responses to Cindy), but rather Dan's use of psychology as the basis for some of his counseling.

We'll return to the story of Cindy, Ralph, and Dan as we continue this chapter, but for now let us look at the realities of life in the last decade of the twentieth century.

We live in a psychological society. That statement probably comes as a surprise to no one. The emergence of humanistic psychology, of self-help books, of all sorts of psychological schools of thought, and all sorts of counseling methods—both secular and Christian—caused one writer to characterize psychology's proliferation as "The Shrinking of America."[1]

Psychology's Effect on the Church

Nowhere has the rise of psychology caused more concern or confusion than in the church. So many books have been written attacking the use of all sorts of psychologies that it would be impossible to list them all. Here is a general sampling:[2] Paul C. Vitz, *Psychology as Religion*; William Kirk Kilpatrick, *Psychological Seduction*; Mark P. Cosgrove, *Psychology Gone Awry*; and Martin and Deidre Bobgan's *The Psychological Way/The Spiritual Way*, which precedes a series of books in which the Bobgans critique what they call "psychoheresy."[3]

Perhaps the most important of all the Christian critiques of psychology was one of the very first. In 1977, Dr. Paul C. Vitz, himself an associate professor of psychology at New York University, issued a trenchant Christian analysis of secular psychology called *Psychology as Religion: The Cult of Self Worship*.[4] The title is telling. His critique is centered primarily on the modern humanistic psychologists: Erich Fromm, Carl

Rogers, Abraham Maslow, and Rollo May. Vitz systematically exposed the self-centered nature of modern secular psychology as emerging from an anti-Christian root—the thought of Ludwig Feuerbach. Feuerbach's *The Essence of Christianity* is anything but an evangelical treatise; rather, as Vitz points out,

> First published in 1841, revised in 1843, this work by a left-wing follower of Hegel became widely known for its influential attack on Christianity. Friedrich Engels described his response to the book, "One must himself have experienced the liberating effect of this book to get an idea of it. Enthusiasm was general; we all became at once Feuerbachians." Among other later thinkers whose ideas about religion were directly or indirectly affected by Feuerbach were Marx, Nietzsche, Huxley, John Stuart Mill, Freud, and Dewey. The tradition of Marx, Nietzsche, and Freud leads to Fromm and May; that of Mill, Huxley and Dewey connects directly to Rogers and Maslow.[5]

Vitz clearly shows the tie between some popular self-help theories and their roots in a nonChristian worldview. Feuerbach said, "That which in religion ranks first—namely, God—is, as I have shown, in truth and reality something second; for God is merely the projected essence of Man. . . . If the nature of Man is man's Highest Being, if to be human is his highest existence, then man's love for Man must in practice become the first and highest law. *Homo homini Deus est*—man's God is MAN." Whatever Feuerbach considered his view, it is anything but a Christ-centered faith; it is anything but Christian in any rational sense.

Another important Christian thinker, Dr. Larry Crabb of the Institute of Biblical Counseling in Morrison, Colorado, has critiqued secular psychology. Crabb's summary of his critique of secular techniques echoes Vitz:

Freud said that man is selfish and one ought to first know it, then accept it as OK. Ego psychology claims that man can be strengthened to successfully rechannel selfishness into personally and socially acceptable outlets. [Carl] Rogers denies any inner badness and teaches that man is filled with goodness and should therefore let it all hang out. Skinner contends that man is neither good nor bad, that he is a complicated mass of responses which in terms of intrinsic value amounts to a large zero. Since man can be controlled, let experts (Skinnerian psychologists) control him toward ends desired ultimately by the controller who himself is totally controlled (a random vicious circle with no breaking in point). Existentialists don't know if man is bad (Freud), good (Rogers), both (ego psychologists), or neither (Skinner). Man is logically absurd but needs something besides rational meaninglessness; therefore leave rationality behind and blindly hope that some experience will fill the void.[6]

Crabb and others have developed extensive models of counseling that are based on the authority and reliability of biblical revelation.[7] The notion that any counseling can be done apart from a Christian world and life view is not present in the writings of these thinkers. In short, there is a stark contrast between the writings of Christian counselors and the writings of the secular theorists they have critiqued.

RALPH'S RESOLUTION

Cindy showed up at "Guadalajara's" as promised. She entered the festive atmosphere of the restaurant promptly at 7 p.m., finding Ralph and Megan seated in the lounge sipping club sodas. The cheery red and blue floor tiles drifted past as the hostess led them into a spacious dining room. They were seated amid brightly colored serape wall hangings. A variety of red, green, and blue chili peppers dangled from the ceiling. For the first few minutes they exchanged pleasantries and mostly allowed each other to brag about their children, nieces, and nephews.

Ralph smiled when Cindy brought out an old photograph of him, and they reminisced about happy times of Bible studies together. Suddenly Ralph sighed, and Megan, sensing some discomfort, softly asked him what was wrong.

"If only I'd known then just a glimmer of the freedom I have in Christ, what a difference it would have made in my teaching, and especially in my counseling."

Cindy perked up and asked, "Ralph, what did you mean this morning, when you said you had been wrong about Dan?"

"Cindy, I was terribly suspicious of Dan when he came. I guess I was overly protective of the church and our 'territory.' As you know, we tried to work out a situation where Dan's counseling ministry would be tied to the church. But many of us on the elder board thought Dan's techniques were way off base biblically. Eventually, we all sensed it just wasn't going to work. He explained his views repeatedly, but we just wouldn't listen. Dan established his practice alone, and as you know, our relationship was strained at best for a long time.

"The turning point came when Mrs. Attenborough brought her granddaughter Lisa to me for counseling. Lisa was the angriest teenager I had ever met. The violent changes in her attitudes made it seem like she was two people. She was suffering badly from anorexia. I tried to help her, as did several others in the church. In exasperation one day, after another counseling session where we made no progress, I took a walk to clear my head. I saw Dan down at McDonald's and asked his opinion about what to do. What has happened since, I must admit, is truly amazing.

"Dan took Lisa on as a client. Slowly but surely, he discovered she had been abused severely by a preschool teacher, sexually and corporally. On top of that, her parents admitted they had overdone their own expectations of her as a child. The pain she experienced had created wounds so deep, which Lisa buried, that she'd developed an incredible distrust of everyone. Her anger was turned inward, and she had come to believe that she was unworthy of love. This led to such an explosiveness that she was truly dangerous to herself and her family. Once she viciously ripped open a classmate's arm with a fingernail file.

"After many months, I began to see that with Dan's help Lisa was making progress. I asked Dan if I could see her and he said he preferred that I not counsel her. This made me angry and I asked him to discuss it with me. We met at 9 a.m. on Dan's day off. I came loaded with my objections to his methods and everything we'd discussed before.

"This time Dan was ready for me. He went straight to what he perceived as the main issue before us. He asked me, if I were to need brain surgery, would I hire a heart specialist? If I needed my car's engine tuned, would I hire a plumber? On both counts I laughed, 'Of course not.'

"'Then why,' Dan asked, 'do you want to counsel an angry anorectic teenager with whom you've already failed?' I must admit, I stammered a bit in response. Dan grinned and said that he suspected I was being territorial. 'Would you,' he asked, 'object if a church member hired a doctor to perform needed surgery? Would you go in and demand to see the diagnosis or wait patiently and let the family decide when to tell you?'

"At that point I learned Dan had gotten both Lisa's and Mrs. Attenborough's permission to discuss Lisa's case with me. The information Dan had was fascinating. I had no idea that 95 percent of the people who suffer from anorexia are women. Dan pointed out that *psychologists* had discovered such things from extensive research. We discussed the value of psychology. Here are the five issues we examined in depth."

At this point Ralph took out a paper and handed it to Cindy. The five issues numbered on the following pages were on that paper. The discussion that follows is Ralph's explanation.

THE MAJOR DISPUTES BETWEEN PSYCHOLOGY AND CHRISTIAN FAITH

One: There Is a Spiritual Way to Counsel That Is Better Than the Psychological Way

"On this point, Dan's response was very interesting. He allowed that modern psychology was often wrong in its prescriptions for problems. But most important, we discussed the vast differences between the various psychological camps.

"The discipline of psychology is not monolithic. You cannot lump everyone who practices psychology into one group and claim that that camp is wrong. Psychologists are like preachers or churches—not all of them preach the same gospel. Some practice their psychology with a careful attention to biblical detail. When these psychologists prescribe help for problems, they utilize biblical insights and wisdom to inform their prescriptions. Likewise, these same people may discover the problem that someone suffers from by utilizing a psychological method of observation.

"Dan observed that a strength of psychology is often in describing the problems from which someone suffers, but it is often weak on the prescription to allay the problem.

"Take an issue like self-image. Modern psychology has been blasted by Christian critics for advocating glorification of self.[8] Yet, at times these critics seem to have misunderstood the purpose of the self-image discussion as carried on in mainstream psychology. Listen to the words of two Christian psychologists," Ralph said as he started to read from his papers:

> Mainstream psychology's position on self-image can be clarified with the analogy of a marksman shooting at a target. A marksman is more concerned with accuracy than with whether the shot is low or high. Concepts of low or high are only used to improve accuracy. Never would a marksman conclude "the higher the better."

Likewise, psychologists have traditionally been interested in accuracy of self-concept. It may be important to observe whether self-image is low or high, but only for the sake of adjusting accuracy. Few psychologists have concluded "the higher the better."

Classical self psychologists made a distinction between accurate self-image and the excessive self-love of narcissism. Allport wrote that inherent narcissism could not be dominant in the psychologically mature person. Fromm, Adler, Maslow, Allport, and Rogers all emphasized that a person with a healthy self-image is rarely selfish. Kilpatrick's perspective that self psychology has obscured a concern for others may be true of some popular psychological writings, but it does not represent mainstream psychology.

In addition to Kilpatrick's mistaken conclusion about what mainstream psychology believes a healthy self-image to be, Hunt and McMahon are also in error. They have confused self-image with narcissism. They note that Paul warned Timothy that in the last days "People will be lovers of themselves" (2 Timothy 3:2), which means selfish. But there is little doubt that Paul himself had a healthy self-image. He wrote frequently of his accomplishments and encouraged his readers to imitate him. But Paul was not narcissistic, focusing on himself to the exclusion of a concern for others. Moses also appeared to develop an accurate self-image as evidenced by his style of leadership.[9]

"Dan observed that is where a solid biblically informed psychologist has the advantage on those who never allow the Scriptures to have a say in their study.

"For example, if a person is to develop an accurate (healthy) self-image, he or she must come to terms with the bad side of human nature. At this point, the work of many

Christian psychologists can be of immense help, for they point us to our basic sin nature. In his book *Inside Out*, Larry Crabb challenges Christians to come to grips with their goals and their own sinful efforts to reach those goals apart from relationship with God. As an example of how the church aids and abets our self-sufficiency, Crabb vividly points out the false promises prevalent in the church today:

> Modern Christianity, in dramatic reversal of its biblical form, promises to relieve the pain of living in a fallen world. . . . The promise of bliss is for NOW! Complete satisfaction can be ours this side of Heaven. . . . The point of living the Christian life has shifted from knowing and serving Christ till He returns to soothing, or at least learning to ignore, the ache in our soul.[10]

"The message is prophetic and profound: *We cannot be truly satisfied or experience true joy apart from a biblical understanding of ourselves*—including our deeply sinful, ugly insides. By seeking God first, down deep, only then can we experience joy in other relationships and, ultimately, any level of satisfaction. Total, blissful satisfaction just isn't available in a fallen, sinful world.

"Not all Christian counseling experts are as realistic as Crabb, but most affirm similar approaches that include healthy doses of the biblical truth about human nature. The key is to find those who do emphasize the Bible and utilize its truth in their practice. It is those counselors who allow that biblical view to inform and control their psychology who are effective. Instead of an either/or approach to counseling, instead of a sharp distinction between the psychological way and the spiritual way, those who begin with a biblical anthropology are able to develop a biblical psychology and apply it effectively in the counseling environment. Like the effective evangelist, this counselor is able to speak the historic truth of the Christian faith into the difficult challenges of a secular culture and a secularized discipline, helping hurting people with complex problems. Instead of tossing out psychology on to its unbiblical ear, this counselor redeems it for the glory of God and the benefit of real people with real needs.

Two: Why Should a Christian Seek Counseling If God Can Meet All Our Needs?

"Dan and I were in agreement on this from the beginning," Ralph pointed out to Cindy. "We just didn't realize we were speaking the same language until we sat down and worked through it.

"We agreed that in Scripture God Himself encourages people to seek counsel. But we still had problems in the area of what kind of counsel a person should seek. Should it have a psychological technique attached?

"Dan pointed out that seeking an appropriate counselor doesn't necessarily mean seeking a psychologist, but that neither should a professional be ruled out. This is a lot like seeking a suitable church or preacher. Some preach the truth of the gospel and some are wolves in sheep's clothing, preaching a false gospel. Some psychologists are godly and base their assumptions about counseling on biblical grounds, while others do not. The question really is, Dan pointed out, whether the person with a particular problem can find a counselor or therapist who shares his or her strong, orthodox Christian values and whether the patient believes this counselor is right for him or her. Even then, however, we have no guarantee of success.[11]

"His final point was that seeking counsel does not deny God's sufficiency to meet our needs, which is a big objection many have to seeking counsel. Rather, God's Word records numerous instances where the Lord Jesus, the apostle Paul, and other New Testament writers actually counseled others. I've already mentioned the admonitions in Proverbs to seek godly counsel, but in 1 Thessalonians 5:14, Paul makes clear the *necessity* of wise counsel for wayward hearts, unseemly behavior, and those who suffer from emotional distress or weakness: "We urge you, brothers, *warn* those who are idle, *encourage* the timid, *help* the weak, *be patient* with everyone" (emphasis added).

In these admonitions there are four implicit suggestions: (1) Christians are God's ambassadors, His agents or servants, available to help meet others' needs. (2) People are going to struggle in this sinful world; they will need counseling. (3) Counseling, even using psychological insights, can benefit both the person counseled and the counselor. (4) And, since God Himself has encouraged us to seek counsel, it must be His way of using His resources to meet important human needs.

Three: Psychology Has Become a Religion that Competes with Christianity

"Certainly," Ralph affirmed, "in the large sense this is true. In every age in every culture in which the Christian faith has been preached, people have searched for idols to replace it. Modern secular psychology has become such an idol for many. But it would be both unwise and irresponsible to conclude that we must reject all of psychology or psychology's research findings just because *some* have used it as a replacement for true Christian faith. As Collins points out,

> Instead of dismissing all psychology as a rival religion, let us evaluate its findings, learn from them and make use of psychology's insights when they are consistent with Scripture. In this way we can use psychological conclusions to help others deal with the complexities of modern living.[12]

"So long as psychological principles and research are subordinated to biblical precepts, and communicated to us by someone more interested in serving the living God than the gods of psychology or academia, then we can be assured of a biblical psychology. Remember, psychology began simply as the study of the mind or soul of man (Greek: *psuche*) and of human behaviors that begin as thoughts or inclinations. The word even has its place in the New Testament (see Matthew 10:28, 16:2; Hebrews 4:12, 6:19; 1 Peter 2:11).

"When Freud and his minions popularized the concepts of psychotherapy and located the origins of bad or 'unhealthy' behavior in the client's family of origin (this is not to diminish the importance of study in this area), the church's main response was to acquiesce to the new and popular theories. Instead of boldly reasserting the doctrine of original sin and the necessity of repentant faith to overcome it, Christendom slowly but surely gave in to describing sin as mere behavioral aberrance and psychological weakness. Again, instead of strategically and courageously seeking to bring the discipline of psychology into the light of Scripture and under the lordship of Christ, the church has allowed it, in its secularized form, to be the chief progenitor of the idols of our age: self, self, and more self! Christians must realize that, counseling is not only an important aspect of biblical ministry, but it has become one of the most influential disciplines in Western culture, and it's fast making inroads into the East.[13]

"At this point, the church must make a strategic 'about-face' and seek—as many Christian psychologists and psychiatrists are faithfully attempting—to bring solid biblical doctrine and insight to psychology and to take advantage of the abundant insights that the discipline has for us. We must pray that those who are faithful to God and to biblical truth can reclaim this discipline, which has origins not merely in understanding human behavior, but in understanding the very souls of men and women.

Four: Are All Emotional Problems Caused by Sin?
Ralph continued, "Martin and Deidre Bobgan have been some of the most outspoken evangelical critics of secular psychology. But on the issue of how we must treat psychological and emotional human problems, they have also provided a penetrat-

ing analysis. They have emphasized the spiritual component of human problems, but were also clear that every problem also has a mental and physical component." Ralph straightened his notes, and began to read from the Bobgans:

> The medical doctor's main interest is with the body and the psychotherapist's with the mind. The separation of mind from body is a naive way of dealing with the total person. . . . The body, mind, and the spirit must be considered in any problem which one is experiencing. . . . Any system which regards one, such as the body or the mind, without considering all three, and particularly the spiritual part of man, falls short of truly ministering to the whole person.[14]

"Counselor Gary Collins affirms this truth as do Larry Crabb and others. Collins gives the example of depression, pointing out that it may be the result of a physical cause (biochemical disorder), the result of stress (loss of job), or the result of sin. His point is well taken:

> The effective Christian counselor knows that personal sin may be a major cause of depression, but it would be simplistic to conclude that treatment should include nothing but finding the sin and exhorting the person to change. Sometimes it is necessary to uncover and treat the physical causes of depression. At times we need to help the counselee cope with his or her psychological stress.[15]

"Christians must be careful not to throw the psychological baby out with the critical bath water. If the person we exhort to change has brain chemistry so out of balance that he finds it impossible to change, we could be endangering his emotional or even physical well-being. Remembering that human problems can and often do have as many as three components will help maintain a balanced approach to counseling.

Five: Should All Counseling Take Place Through the Local Church?

Ralph continued: "Most evangelical leaders—even those heavily involved in teaching psychology and counseling—would affirm the value of having many if not most of the counseling needs of church members taken care of in the local church.[16] Collins points out three important conclusions about lay counseling:

1. Lay counseling can and does help people.
2. Lay counseling is not the panacea for all human problems.
3. Lay counseling should be an important part of the church's work and ministry.[17]

"However, as Collins himself points out, there are clear limits to what lay counselors can accomplish. There will always be a need for professionals who are able to perform 'the psychological equivalent of brain surgery.'

"Because many people have suffered serious abuse—as you know personally, Cindy—or may have other serious disorders, lay counselors should be trained to recognize their limits in helping people deal with problems. However, the lay counselor may be an invaluable help in supporting the progress of the counselee and the work of the psychologist in such cases."

CONCLUSION

"Well, Cindy," Ralph said, "I guess you can see I'm changing my thinking a bit on these things."

Cindy nodded in agreement and couldn't contain her smile. "Ralph," she said, "I really never thought I'd see this day, but I'm glad it's here. Now about my being absent from First Church so much lately. . . ."

Chapter Six

THE CONTROVERSY OVER THE HEALTH AND WEALTH GOSPEL

❖

Would you rather be rich than poor or middle class? Would you rather drive a new luxury car, say a Cadillac, Mercedes, or Lexus, or a fancy van, than your aging Chevrolet or Toyota? Wouldn't you enjoy having $100,000 in the bank rather than living paycheck to paycheck and seeing your savings grow only $100 a month (or less)? Most of us, if we're honest, would probably rather have newer cars, clothes, and homes, and it would be even more appealing if we knew that having such things was God's will!

The message of a growing minority of rather vocal leaders within the charismatic movement is that God wants us healthy and wealthy. A number of writers have recently expressed serious concerns about these developments.

THE CRISIS IN THE CHARISMATIC MOVEMENT

D. R. McConnell, a professor at Oral Roberts University, warns that the charismatic movement is facing a major crisis. The movement, he states, is at a crossroads that will determine whether it remains faithful to the Bible or becomes cultic. In his words, "The charismatic renewal has reached a spiritual intersection in its history, and the decisions made by charismatic leadership in the next five years will, I believe, forever determine our place in the annals of church history. Nothing less than the doctrinal orthodoxy of our movement is at stake."[1] McConnell continues, there is much "that passes for 'truth' in the charismatic renewal that I believe deeply grieves the Holy Spirit, who is 'the Spirit of truth.' I would go so far as to say that many in the present charismatic renewal preach and practice a different gospel."[2] McConnell, it should be noted, is a strong advocate of charismatic renewal.

McConnell's challenge is directed at the fastest growing segment of the charismatic movement, namely, those independent churches and ministries that teach what critics often call "the Health and Wealth Gospel" or "Name It and Claim It." Proponents of the teaching reject such labels, prefering such names as "the Word Movement" or "the Word of Faith Movement."

The Word of Faith Donation Factories: Religious Trash?

The best known representatives of the word of faith movement include Kenneth Hagin, Kenneth and Gloria Copeland, Robert Tilton, Fred Price, Charles Capps, Jerry Savelle, Marilyn Hickey, Norvel Hayes, and W. V. Grant. Their television ministries, personal appearances, and publications enable them to reach huge audiences that support their ministries with millions of dollars every year.

USA Today recently identified Robert Tilton as "the USA's fastest-growing force in TV evangelism."[3] Contributions to his ministry alone, the paper reports, easily exceed 25 million dollars annually. The same story in *USA Today* reveals why evangelicals ought to be concerned with Tilton's brand of TV evangelism, which millions of people equate with the broader evangelical movement. "In return for a '$1,000 vow,'" the paper reports that Tilton claims his prayers will "cast out demons, cure disease and yield cash and shiny new cars for the truly faithful."[4]

Jeffrey Haddan, a University of Virginia sociologist who specializes in TV evangelism, states that Tilton has "gone well beyond the prosperity gospel . . . and crossed the line into a sham." Haddan describes Tilton's TV show as "religious trash."[5] Whatever it is, it is an approach to health and wealth that too many people will necessarily associate with the evangelical mainstream, which of course deplores what Tilton represents.

Most recently, on *Prime Time Live* (ABC) on November 21, 1991, Tilton and W. V. Grant were both exposed as frauds. The *Prime Time* episode incited investigations by the Texas Attorney General's office and the Internal Revenue Service.[6] In fairness to Tilton, he has successfully filed and received restraining orders against the Texas Attorney General and that investigation may be on hold indefinitely.

According to *Prime Time*'s Diane Sawyer, Tilton's ministry takes in over $80 million a year, and since 1985, Tilton's salary has been at least $400,000 a year. The report claimed that Tilton has access to more than $60 million in assets, including four luxury homes in Texas, Florida, and California.

The most damning portion of the program concerned Tilton's claim to care deeply for the hurting people among his followers. Yet, the *Prime Time* exposé showed that most of Tilton's mail—full of prayer requests and sincere needs from those very hurting followers—had been found in the trash dumpster behind Tilton's bank in Tulsa, Oklahoma. The evidence seemed to indicate that Tilton had never seen the prayer requests, but the checks from the envelopes had certainly made it into his bank account. This prompted Diane Sawyer to label Tilton's word of faith ministry a "state-of-the-art donation factory."[7]

A Lack of Accountability
In the word of faith movement, we are seeing individuals who, for the most part, operate apart from the standards and constraints provided by recognized denominations and agencies created to hold ministries accountable (like the Evangelical

Council for Finance Accountability, ECFA). The people I've identified belong to a loose-knit organization called the International Convention of Faith Churches and Ministries that began in 1979. It presently includes about 100 churches and 700 ministers. But there appear to be few of the checks and balances that a recognized denomination like the Assemblies of God and other pentecostal organizations provide.

Many independent charismatic churches and ministries are either owned by the leaders who started them or are effectively controlled by boards where the leaders and family members control a majority of the votes. The *Prime Time Live* episode also pointed out that Tilton, for example, has claimed he is held accountable by his board. However, it revealed his "board" consists of only himself, his wife, and his secretary. The absence of accountability and controls in such a situation is an open invitation to abuse. The situation is made even worse by the fact that the exaggerated emphasis on subjective feelings often leads to a de-emphasis upon the objective truth revealed in the Bible and located in clearly written doctrinal statements.

Not long ago Benny Hinn, an Orlando pastor and figurehead of a nation-wide TV ministry and author of the best-selling book *Good Morning Holy Spirit*,[8] admitted that he had become part of the word of faith movement and that he had preached false doctrine.[9] As I'll detail later in this chapter, Rev. Hinn acknowledged his errors—something other faith preachers refuse to do. Hinn attributes his doctrinal errors to his lack of serious Bible training, which he said he intends to correct.[10]

Many leaders of independent charismatic churches are in a state of educational impoverishment. They are undereducated in such standard areas as the liberal arts and sciences but also in critical fields for leaders in Christian ministry: biblical studies, systematic theology, and church history. It is at least possible that the reason why some of them get swayed into heretical teaching is because they have no serious acquaintance with the truth. It's difficult to recognize the counterfeit when you aren't acquainted with the real thing.

A Summary of the Crisis

What we have, then, is a situation in which poorly educated people have assumed control over massive ministries that reach millions of people over the airwaves and hundreds of thousands more live and in-person. Don't get me wrong, I recognize that a person does not have to have a college or seminary education to serve God. And I'm not advocating some sort of new gnosticism—special enlightenment—for those who do serve the Savior. But it has been a well-established tenet of historic, orthodox Christian faith for centuries that its leadership seek the best education they can find.

One other unfortunate thing that the *Prime Time Live* episode revealed was in an interview with an alleged college sidekick of Robert Tilton's. This man, who refused to be identified and was disguised for the camera, claimed that he and Tilton, during their college years, would get drunk and go to evangelistic tent meetings where they would claim to be in the Spirit and speak in tongues. From these experiences, the mystery guest explained, he and Tilton actually planned to purchase a tent after college and fly around the country conducting similar meetings in order to get rich! As the *Prime Time Live* segment pointed out, however, Tilton never finished college. It implied he did find the time to buy that tent and get rich.

To summarize the evidence and the concerns pointed out by the *Prime Time Live* episode and those of responsible charismatic leaders such as McConnell, here are the main, troublesome features of the word of faith movement:

1. A lack of appropriate education in the leadership.
2. A lack of accountability and internal controls.
3. No one within the fellowship to challenge abuses of power such as diversions of contributions to

> build expensive homes or purchase luxury automobiles for personal use.

As we'll see, however, there are further dimensions to the problem that are, to mainstream evangelicals, even more disturbing.

When these self-appointed leaders take their frequently confused message to the world by means of television, we should not be surprised at the doctrinal chaos that results. The situation is made even more regrettable when people in the media identify TV preachers of this sort with responsible representatives of the gospel or with the evangelical mainstream.

Why do people follow such leaders in such large numbers? One reason may be the language they use. No doubt, some who listen to these preachers are themselves biblically and theologically unaware or misinformed. They hear the preachers use familiar biblical passages as proof-texts; they hear familiar evangelical and pentecostal terminology used. Because the packaging is familiar, they fall into the trap of thinking that the content of the message can be trusted.

Word of faith leaders also preach an extremely attractive message. In the words of Charles Farah, the teaching of the faith movement is "without question the most attractive message being preached today or, for that matter, in the whole history of the Church."[11]

"Seldom if ever," writes D. R. McConnell, "has there been a gospel that has promised so much, and demanded so little. . . . The Faith gospel promises health and long life to a world in which death can come a myriad of different ways."[12]

There can be no question about the extent to which the word of faith movement is dividing the contemporary church, evangelicalism as a whole, and the pentecostal/charismatic branches of evangelicalism. Let's now examine what the movement teaches about divine healing, prosperity, and positive confession. Then we'll take a look at recent charges that some leaders of the movement are teaching heresy.

THE WORD OF FAITH VIEW OF DIVINE HEALING

Is It Classic Pentecostalism?

Kenneth Hagin speaks for the entire word of faith movement when he states, "I believe that it is the plan of God our Father that no believer should ever be sick."[13] Word of faith leaders teach something that sounds initially like the classical pentecostal view that healing is in the atonement. According to that teaching, Christ's atonement had more than just the forgiveness of sin as a goal; it also secures physical healing from disease for the believer. But many faith preachers place a significantly different twist on the old doctrine of divine healing.

Like Kenneth Hagin, they believe that Christ's spiritual atonement in hell, and not His physical death on the cross, is the basis for this healing. Since, on this view, all physical disease has a *spiritual cause*, Christians must therefore seek a *spiritual cure*. This has made it easy for some in the movement to believe that illness is "all in the head." Some critics of the movement have charged that this view is distressingly similar to the teaching of Christian Science. They also argue that it can lead deceived followers into thinking that medical science can or even should be ignored. After all, as D. R. McConnell points out, "Medicine is a *physical* science. The whole science of medicine is based on the ability to detect, diagnose, and prescribe treatment of disease and its symptoms. Because the Faith teachers believe that disease is *spiritual* . . . they must, by definition, also consider the *physical* science of medicine an inferior means of healing."[14]

This leads to the dangerous consequence that, for the word of faith teachers, it is more important to deny physical symptoms than it is to detect them. "The physical symptoms are not real" for people under the spell of this teaching, McConnell warns. The physical symptoms become real when the believer's faith has wavered. "Only people who do not know how to believe God for *spiritual* healing resort to medical science."[15]

In fairness, it should be noted that not all representatives of the faith teaching advise people to avoid medical science. They claim to believe in good doctors. But even in cases where medical science is tolerated, it appears to function as a stop-gap measure until the healing of faith can begin. Nevertheless, critics have charged that the movement's frequent rejection of medical science can result in situations when its followers fail to seek necessary medical help. In some instances, followers of this teaching have died of preventable causes.[16] All of this is a marked departure from the healing ministries of individuals like Oral Roberts and Kathryn Kuhlman, neither of whom rejected medical science.

They Claim Healing Is "an Accomplished Fact"

Another distinctive feature of the word of faith teaching is its claim that the believer's physical healing is already completed, an accomplished *fact*. The catch, unfortunately, is that this "accomplished fact" is a "faith-fact." This means that the healing is often not yet evident through any termination of the physical symptoms in the follower's body. This suggests that the physical symptoms should be denied, that in some sense they are not real. Once again, the resemblance to Christian Science is unsettling. Such teaching can lead to obvious abuse. Don Carson explains:

> The most common form of abuse is the view that since all illness is directly or indirectly attributable to the devil and his works, and since Christ by his cross has defeated the devil, and by his Spirit has given us the power to overcome him, healing is the inheritance right of all true Christians who call upon the Lord with genuine faith. The entailment, of course, is that if someone is not healed, the failure reflects inadequate faith, since the promises of the Lord are not to be called into doubt.[17]

James Packer has written critically about the appeal the word of faith movement (and similar teaching in other pentecostal and charismatic groups) has for people who believe "that God means us to spend our time in this fallen world feeling well and in a state of euphoria based on that fact."[18]

Packer counters this by pointing out how "New Testament references to unhealed sickness among Christian leaders make it plain that good health at all times is not God's will for all believers." He also refers to "the charismatic supposition of reality without bitterness when Christians are exposed to the discipline of pain and of remaining unhealed."[19]

The apostle Paul teaches that our outer man is decaying (2 Corinthians 4:16). While we groan in this body, God's Spirit is His pledge of the new body that awaits us at the resurrection (2 Corinthians 5:1-5). Paul was unable to heal associates like Epaphroditus (Colossians 4:14), Timothy (1 Timothy 5:23), and Trophimus (2 Timothy 4:20). Paul himself suffered from physical illness (Galatians 4:13-15, 2 Timothy 12:7-9). Luke, the author of the third gospel and the book of Acts, was a physician (Colossians 4:14).

CHRISTIANITY IS NO HEALING CULT

D. R. McConnell warns against turning Christianity into some kind of healing cult. In his words, "Christianity is not a healing cult and the gospel is not a metaphysical formula for divine health and wealth. The Faith theology's inordinate emphasis on healing is a gross exaggeration of the biblical doctrine and distorts the centrality of Christ and the gospel."[20] For word of faith preachers, McConnell cautions, "healing is not a sovereign miracle bestowed by a merciful God. Healing is a cause-and-effect formula that works every time the Christian applies it in 'faith.' "[21]

Anytime some Christian leaders tells us what God *must* do, warning alarms should start going off all over the place. McConnell's observation is certainly right:

Those who use healing formulas to claim that God heals *all* our diseases *every* time are denying reality. They are ignoring the obvious fact that Christians get sick all the time. Some recover from their illnesses; others do not. Every day, somewhere in the world, Christians die of the same diseases that everybody else dies of. This is not a pleasant fact, but it is an undeniable one. If we deny it, then we deny not only reality, but also what the Bible itself has said of life in this physical body.[22]

The word of faith teaching regarding healing is suspect for a number of reasons: It clashes with what the Bible teaches about pain and disease; it deceives Christians into often rejecting medical help; it misleads Christians into thinking that the continuance of disease reflects the presence of sin and unbelief in their hearts; and it leads the church dangerously close to the heresies of the Christian Science movement. This is a teaching that biblically informed Christians will shun.

PROSPERITY: CORNERSTONE
OF THE HEALTH AND WEALTH MOVEMENT

So far, we have examined the health component of the so-called "Health and Wealth Gospel." Let's now turn our attention to the movement's emphasis on prosperity, which it claims is God's will for all believers.

Kenneth Copeland summarizes his view of the doctrine of prosperity in these words:

We must understand that there are laws governing every single thing in existence. Nothing is by accident. There are laws of the world of the spirit and there are laws of the world of the natural. . . . We need to realize that the spiritual world and its laws are more powerful

than the physical world and its laws. Spiritual laws
gave birth to physical law. . . . The same rule is true in
prosperity. There are certain laws governing prosperity
in God's Word. Faith causes them to function.[23]

Key Texts for the Prosperity Doctrine

Gloria Copeland teaches that Mark 10:29-30 "gives us, if we
have enough faith to receive it, the right to believe for a return of
one thousand dollars on a ten-dollar contribution."[24] But Mrs.
Copeland conveniently neglects the fact that Mark 10:29-30
*follows immediately after another passage that warns against
the spiritual dangers of riches* (see 10:25). Jesus' promise in
Mark 10:29-30 specifically dealt with things that no one would
necessarily expect a one-hundredfold return on: "No one who
has left home or brothers or sisters or mother or father or children or fields for me and the gospel will fail to receive a hun-
dred times as much in this present age (homes, brothers, sisters,
mothers, children and fields—and with them, persecutions) and
in the age to come, eternal life."

Another phrase that is often cited by advocates of the prosperity doctrine is in 3 John 2: "that thou mayest prosper" (KJV).
But according to pentecostal scholar Gordon Fee, John's words
are simply the usual way friends at that time in history greeted
each other in letters. The *New International Version* translates
the phrase, "that all may go well with you." There is absolutely
no justification for the contemporary use of this phrase in the
prosperity teaching of the faith preachers.

Sub-Christian Teaching

The prosperity doctrine is a clear example of sub-Christian teaching. It catches the fancy of contemporary people drawn to a message that promises them a life of ease. In this case, the message
reduces to the belief that if we serve God, we'll get rich.

While we should welcome any effort to get Christians to
bring their needs before God and to search God's Word with

regard to His promises, the word of faith preachers clearly use the word *need* in a sense far broader than anything found in Scripture. As McConnell points out,

> If we accept the dictionary definition that a need is something without which we will die or no longer be able to function, then we would have to say that the Faith teachers have gone far beyond the confines of even the English language. New houses, fancy cars, and fine clothing hardly qualify as "needs," as items without which we will surely perish. The doctrine of prosperity fails to make any distinction between a *need* and a *want* and a *want* and a *lust.*[25]

Judged by the standards of the teaching of the word of faith movement, the apostle Paul never achieved its kind of prosperity. Paul could only write,

> We have been made a spectacle to the whole universe. . . . We are weak, but you are strong! You are honored, we are dishonored! To this very hour we go hungry and thirsty, we are in rags, we are brutally treated, we are homeless. We work hard with our own hands. When we are cursed, we bless; when we are persecuted, we endure it; when we are slandered, we answer kindly. Up to this moment we have become the scum of the earth, the refuse of the world. (1 Corinthians 4:9-13)

Yet Robert Tilton has proclaimed on several occasions, "being poor is a sin,"[26] and "the only time people were poor in the Bible, is when they were under a curse."[27] Surely Paul was not under a curse when he wrote 1 Corinthians 4:9-13!

By appealing to a common human weakness, word of faith teachers debase the very gospel they claim to represent. It is a teaching that thoughtful believers must dismiss.

THE POSITIVE CONFESSION DOCTRINE

According to James Goff, Jr., word of faith preachers believe that "divine health and prosperity are the rights of every Christian who will appropriate enough faith to receive them. The secret of appropriating such faith is in making a 'positive confession'—that is, stating in faith what one desires or is requesting from God and believing that God will honor it."[28]

The doctrine of *positive confession* functions as a foundation for the health and wealth emphases of the word of faith teaching. As William Menzies explains, positive confession is "the belief that a believer's verbal assertion of a desired objective, affirmed in faith, *requires* God to bring that objective into being. Extreme forms of this teaching have led followers to believe that wealth and health are the badges of faith."[29]

It is hard to miss the unbiblical implication of all this. Word of faith preachers act as though God is somehow required to do certain things when the believer issues prayerful commands. In such a view, "God becomes akin to a 'cosmic bellhop,' rather than the Sovereign of the Universe."[30] It is hard to know whether a theology that views God as a servile butler is blasphemy or nonsense. But the result, Goff asserts, "is human pride and a faulty view of both the purpose for, and the relationship between, God and believers. Critics not only accuse the faith teachers of distorting Scripture by taking verses out of context to prove their theology but also point out that there is an explicit rejection of believers who do not get healed or suffer the indignity of poverty, since the only assumption can be that they fail to appropriate faith in God to remedy their situation."[31]

To complete this section, D. R. McConnell summarizes the roots and fruits of the positive confession teaching:

> Many regard this [positive confession] as a healthy practice, emphasizing the psychological benefits of positive thinking and speaking. What this fails to consider

is the historical fact that those who first taught PMA [positive mental attitude]/positive confession—the New Thought metaphysicians—attributed its power to cosmic principles and occultic deities. Though the Bible does emphasize the importance of a pure mind and holy speech, it nowhere states that a person can alter physical reality through mental means, and it certainly does not encourage verbal confession of the divine Name and Word as means of manipulating God's will. In fact, the Scriptures strictly contradict both.[32]

CHARGES OF HERESY

While positive confession and the health and wealth gospel are distortions of biblical teaching, nothing we have noticed thus far comes close to being as serious as the set of charges to be noted in this section. A 1990 book published by Moody Press helped to focus nationwide attention on the theological aberrations of some leaders of the faith movement. Writing in the foreword to the book *The Agony of Deceit*, Harold Lindsell warned that "a number of televangelists are parading under false colors. Historic orthodoxy is being diminished by heretical departures from the true faith over the airwaves."[33] According to the contributors to this book, some of the fastest growing TV ministries are the most heretical. The book should not be read as an indictment of the entire pentecostal and charismatic movements, most of whose leaders are also concerned about the doctrinal deviations of some televangelists. The message of the book is that the real but hitherto largely ignored scandal of TV evangelism is not sexual immorality or luxurious dog houses or financial improprieties. It is heresy!

Suspicious Roots, Metaphysical Fruits
In his book on the word of faith movement, D. R. McConnell criticizes it because of what he sees as its threat to the doctrinal integrity of the historic pentecostal movement.[34] Accord-

ing to McConnell, this movement does not have its roots in historic pentecostalism. Rather, he argues, much of its inspiration arises from the theories of Kenneth Hagin. According to McConnell, Hagin has plagiarized many of his views from others, most notably E. W. Kenyon (1867–1948), an eccentric New England preacher. Kenyon's links to such heretical movements as Unity, Unitarianism, and Christian Science have been documented by McConnell. "What Kenyon produced," William Menzies observes, "is in fact a syncretism of New Thought metaphysics (mind over matter) and radical fundamentalism—a different gospel."[35]

Another area where the suspicious theology of some word of faith leaders shows up is in their distortion of the historic Christian view of divine special revelation. Evangelicalism rejects any and all efforts to locate allegedly "new" revelations outside the canon of the Bible. But a number of faith preachers point to "a direct way of knowing truth that on occasion appears to contradict the teachings of the Bible."[36]

R. C. Sproul warns that Robert Tilton apparently sees himself as "a twentieth-century apostle whose visions of revelation exceed that of the apostle John and whose miracle powers surpass that of the apostle Paul. If we are to believe Tilton's astonishing claims, there is no reason we should not include his writings in the next edition of the New Testament."[37] Along these same lines, William Menzies gives this explanation, "Some extreme faith teachers advocate that esoteric experiences may furnish additional truth to supplement scriptural revelation, thereby implying that such contemporary 'revelations' have apparent validity to the Scriptures."[38]

A Confession by Benny Hinn

In this connection, it is interesting to note admissions made by Benny Hinn that during the 1970s his early ministry was influenced by books written by such strong evangelical thinkers as Dwight Moody and Reuben A. Torrey. But about the time Hinn established his Orlando Christian Center in 1983, a ministry that averages 7,000 people in its Sunday services, he began to follow certain teachings of the word of faith movement. Hinn admitted that he had taught some strange doctrines since that time, including the claim "that each person of the Trinity was a triune being,"[39] a statement that implies nine Persons in the Godhead.

Hinn reportedly acknowledged how "dumb" that teaching was, and he repudiates it. According to *Christianity Today*, which reported the story, "Critics were also dismayed by Hinn's claims that he received some of his controversial teachings via 'revelation knowledge,' or directly from God." Hinn wants "to shed the image of a prophet and that he [will] no longer claim revelation knowledge as the authority for his teachings. Said Hinn, 'The only revelation knowledge is already in the Bible.' "[40]

New evidence has come to light, however, that suggests that Benny Hinn's apparent willingness to submit to correction on his doctrinal failings may be on hold. In the October 5, 1992 issue of *Christianity Today*, several critics are quoted to the effect that the "new" Benny Hinn is out and the "same old Benny Hinn" is back. The article quotes one author as stating that Benny Hinn "has not only bludgeoned Scripture, but has also left in his trail the broken lives of people who have unwittingly fallen for his seductive suggestions."[41] The article cites a number of recent cases in which Hinn has apparently distorted the truth. A number of Hinn's critics see a definite pattern of behavior that raises serious questions about Hinn and his ministry.

Many evangelicals are relieved that one representative of the word of faith movement has at least admitted doctrinal errors, especially with regard to the Trinity and special revelation. But Hinn's admissions only reinforce the concerns about the serious doctrinal errors that continue to appear in the teachings of other faith preachers. When self-appointed prophets lead people to think their teachings, dreams, and visions are revelation and are as authoritative as Scripture, the preachers reveal more than their shallow grounding in theology. Their actions suggest that they are knowingly teaching heresy.

The Final Straw: Copeland's "Little Gods" Doctrine

Rod Rosenbladt claims to have uncovered evidence of a heretical view of Jesus in the preaching and writing of Kenneth Copeland.[42] Copeland has taught that while Jesus was on earth, He was nothing more than a man empowered by God's Spirit. Copeland's belief that the earthly Jesus had abandoned His divine powers resembles the heresy known as Kenoticism. Copeland actually has claimed that he could have done the same thing Jesus did on the cross. It is a mistake to think, Copeland claims, that the wonders Jesus performed result from His possessing powers that we don't have.

All of this leads Copeland to his "little gods" doctrine in which he teaches that "*the believer is as much an incarnation as was Jesus of Nazareth.*"[43] In this matter, Copeland seems to be following Kenneth Hagin who reports that when he was born of God, he "became a human-divine being!"[44] Paul Crouch of the Trinity Broadcasting Network has jumped on this "little gods" bandwagon. On one of his televised programs, he stated, "I am a little god. I have His name. I am one with Him."[45]

It is sobering to realize that, thus far, only one marginal representative of the word of faith movement (Benny Hinn) has admitted his doctrinal errors and, at least in part, broken ties to the movement. Others steadfastly refuse to address the charges of doctrinal error. Some have been heard to say that they will consider the charges only when their critics have as many followers as they do. The rest remain silent.

CONCLUSION

Compared to what we've encountered in this chapter, Christian disagreements over such things as the tribulation and theonomy seem trivial. Those disputes do not begin to affect the heart of the gospel, the essential core teaching of historic Christianity. But preaching that follows the patterns outlined in this chapter is a different story. As Michael Horton observes, "It is to trivialize greatly the work of Christ to suggest that God the Father sent His only-begotten Son into the world to bear the world's blasphemy, insults, and violence, and most of all, to bear the Father's wrath—all for increased cash flow and fewer bouts with asthma."[46] Claims that "Jesus is no longer the only begotten Son of God"[47] sound as heretical as anything taught by any cult in this century.

If these New Age televangelists have been misunderstood, it is time that they tell us whose side they're really on; it is time that they correct the misleading teachings that can so easily confuse their followers; it is time that they show us they not only believe in the historic doctrines of the Trinity and the Incarnation but that they can also explain the doctrines correctly. Until they do these things, committed evangelicals will have to regard them as outside the Christian camp.

Chapter Seven

THE CONTROVERSY OVER CHRISTIAN INVOLVEMENT IN POLITICS

❖

E ach of the great divides examined in this book is important. But the controversial subject of this chapter may be the most serious threat to the unity of the church in the decade ahead. This chapter is important for at least four reasons.

First, entirely too many Christians are indifferent to the great political and social issues of the day. Such indifference may have been easier to understand thirty or forty years ago. The world was a different place then. In that quite different situation, Christian parents were concerned by a sexual and moral permissiveness in society that seems almost tame today by comparison. Drugs and violence in the schools were seldom a problem. The schools taught what schools were designed to teach. Any teacher distributing condoms would have been fired.

But today, there is a cultural and religious war going on as the state seeks to impose values alien to Christians upon society. Further, society frequently coerces Christians in ways that violate their values and religious liberties. In the context of this cultural war, Christian social pacifism betrays the biblical injunction for Christians to act as salt in a decaying society. All that is required for evil people to triumph is for good men and women to do nothing.

Second, many socially active Christians lack a solid understanding of the social, political, philosophical, and economic issues that underlie effective public policy. It is one thing to care about the poor and desire to help them in meaningful ways. But if we misunderstand the foundational issues, we risk supporting policies that will result in more harm being done to the poor.[1]

Reason number three: The church in the United States is becoming increasingly polarized as Christian social activists divide along liberal and conservative lines. Christians must understand why these sharp disagreements exist and explore the possibilities of narrowing these differences.

Finally, some Christians not only refuse to get involved with social and political issues but actually condemn other believers who do. I learned recently about a member of a Baptist church in upstate New York who decided to run for political office. Apparently angered by such a display of what was viewed as backsliding, some wanted the church to vote to exclude this person from holding any church office. Members of another theologically conservative church objected to their pastor's urging Christians to stand in lines alongside of others protesting the evil of abortion. For these Christians, such behavior was "reprehensible" because believers would be cooperating with people deemed insufficiently orthodox.

In this chapter, I argue for the necessity and urgency of Christian involvement in the great social and political debates of our day. I also seek to help the reader understand the growing split in the Body of Christ over social and political issues.

THE GENERAL BACKGROUND OF CHRISTIAN INVOLVEMENT IN POLITICS

Christians and Political/Social Action

Christians need to realize that it is at the point of how we relate to our culture and society that the believer acts out his or her worldview. The Christian worldview does not merely tell us what we should believe about God, the Bible, and salvation from sin, it also tells us how we should live out our beliefs. If unborn babies are human beings, for example, then ending the lives of the unborn is murder.[2] That is the sphere of belief. But if abortion is murder, then Christians are obliged to *do* something. And we can hardly ignore the way various politicians, for whom we are asked to vote, stand on this important issue.

Of course, abortion is not the only issue that should influence our political activity. Just as some political votes end up supporting acts of murder, others support acts of theft, support injustice, or harm the innocent in other ways. One example of injustice, many Christians believe, are efforts on the part of many to deny parents the freedom to choose private schools for their children without the enormous burden of double-taxation.[3] Surely Christians who continue to believe that their faith precludes them somehow from "getting involved in politics" or at least voting their conscience are not considering all the facts.

The Two Sides of Christian Social Activism

There are two sides to Christian social activism. Simply put: we need to care; we need to become involved. That is one side of the issue. But we must also become *informed* social activists! When Christian concern for the poor, for example, is uninformed and thus leads believers to support bad public policy, the result will be even worse consequences for the poor. Some have argued that the trillion or so dollars that the United States has spent "fighting" poverty in the past twenty-five years has often been channeled in bad directions that have made the lives of the poor worse. Such policies have made millions of the poor dependent on welfare, have reduced the incentive of the poor to better themselves, and have encouraged the appalling increase in illegitimate births.

One encouraging feature of the current evangelical movement is the way evangelical scholars have addressed the foundational issues and have sought to provide thinking Christians the basic information about economics, political theory, and social theory.[4]

The Necessity of Involvement

While some theologically conservative Christians disdain social involvement, it is helpful to remember that the church has frequently been at the forefront of the battle against social evils. In the nineteenth century, for example, the Christian William Wilberforce helped lead the fight for important social reforms in Great Britain. In our own day, evangelical leaders like James Dobson (children's issues), Gary Bauer (family issues), and Chuck Colson (prison reform) provide important leadership on vital social issues. Many Americans are active helping millions of impoverished people in Eastern Europe and the former Soviet Union recover from the devastating legacy of communism.

But, some Christians counter, should not our hearts be centered elsewhere than on this world? Certainly. But just as Jesus told us that our treasure should be in heaven, He also commanded us to be the salt of the earth. In biblical times, salt was used as a preservative to retard the spread of decay and corruption. Christians have a biblical mandate to act in ways that will resist the devil in his efforts to expand his influence throughout society. This means we must pay attention to what is occurring in government, in the schools, and in our society. And it means that we must resist evil whenever it threatens.

A MAP OF EVANGELICAL POLITICAL POSITIONS

The following chart serves as a helpful introduction to the range of political options presently found among people who claim to be evangelicals.

The Evangelical Left	The Evangelical Center		The Evangelical Right
The Far Left	Moderate Liberals	Moderate Conservatives	The Far Right

Of course, the chart is referring to *political* differences among evangelical Christians. To call someone a moderate liberal in this context is not necessarily descriptive of that person's theology. Some people are moderate conservatives in their political views while their theological views are left of center. Political views are one thing; theology is another.

The Evangelical Right
There is one good reason why it is probably permissible to say less about the evangelical Christian right in this book. It is impossible to be informed about American society these days without bumping into references about the so-called religious right every day on television, in movies, and in newspapers. If asked to name some representatives of the religious right, few Americans would hesitate before mentioning Jerry Falwell, Pat Robertson, and perhaps one or two others.

While the evangelical religious right gets plenty of attention from the media, almost all of that attention is negative, and sometimes downright hostile. The religious right, we are supposed to believe, is a refuge for social misfits who threaten almost everything Americans hold dear.

There *are* extremists on the right; or at least the fanatics I'll be mentioning are characterized this way. This group includes people who support totalitarianism or racism (such as the Ku Klux Klan) or hold bizarre conspiracy theories (such as members of the John Birch Society). No conservative whom I know regards extremists like this as representatives of conservatism. Regrettably, many people in positions of influence attempt to characterize any Christian, certainly any conservative Christian, as indistinguishable from the far right. Hollywood and the media play this dishonest game all the time.

Practically all members of what could be called the religious right occupy positions somewhere between the evangelical center and some point that is far short of the extreme right. None of them threaten democracy or religious diversity in America.[5]

What beliefs characterize the religious right? Without question, these people believe and defend the historic Christian faith. They believe in the major doctrines of the historic faith, they hold a high view of the Bible, they believe in the importance of a conversion experience called the new birth, and they believe in evangelism, that is, sharing the good news of the gospel with anyone interested in hearing it.

To say that they are politically conservative means they value the form of government expressed in the United States Constitution. They are suspicious of efforts to expand governmental power and control over individuals and such voluntary communities as churches. They are especially concerned about what they see as ill-conceived attempts to use governmental agencies, including the public schools, to weaken or even attack fundamental family values. These people are generally pro-life, although that fact in itself does not always set them apart from moderate Christian liberals. Increasingly, moderate conservatives are recognizing the urgency of school choice as an issue. They have good reasons, they think, to believe that giving every family the right to send their children to any school they wish, including private religious schools, is a necessary step in rescuing American education from mediocrity and amoralism.[6] I'll say more about the evangelical right later in this chapter.

The Evangelical Left
Not surprisingly, one quick way to distinguish the religious left from its counterpart on the right is by political party. Unless the Republican Party does something stupid or the Democratic Party undergoes a change akin to the Russian Revolution of 1991, evangelical conservatives will tend to identify with Republican positions and evangelical liberals will continue to identify with Democratic programs.

Because the religious right is better known than the religious left, later sections of this chapter provide more information about evangelical liberals. For now, it is sufficient to say that these are people who were happy to identify themselves with the policies of George McGovern, Jimmy Carter, Walter Mondale, and Michael Dukakis. Moderate evangelical liberals who professed support for the pro-life position nonetheless supported these pro-abortion presidential candidates. The presidential campaign of 1992 produced no surprises from any representatives of the religious left or right.

The Evangelical Center

My chart has a spot called "the evangelical center." Some might think it a simple matter to identify the view in the middle. Once done, we could issue a simple plea to all the people on the right and left to abandon their eccentric positions and join all the sensible people in the middle. Regrettably, life is not quite that simple.

In theology, there is an identifiable evangelical mainstream.[7] If someone wavers on the essential matter of the Trinity or the deity of Christ or His resurrection or the inspiration and authority of the Bible, then that person has effectively ceased to be an evangelical; he has abandoned the evangelical mainstream.

In the arena of politics and social theory, identifying the center or mainstream is much more difficult. One reason for this difficulty is the fact that both the right and the left believe that their position *is* the mainstream. A dyed-in-the-wool conservative, for example, doesn't really think of himself as off somewhere on the right. He believes that his view represents the mainstream or where the mainstream would be if people were thinking straight. Likewise, liberals are anxious to capture the mainstream for their own positions. Generally speaking, liberals seem to have a great deal more success doing this than do conservatives. Liberals are helped in this, no doubt, by repeated messages to this effect from the liberal media.

I realize there may be skeptics in my audience who think that surely it must be possible to reach a position that is neither left nor right. But is it? Suppose someone seeking to be in the mainstream thought he could do this by denying *every* conservative position. Would the pro-abortion, big government, anti-business, anti-school choice, radical environmentalist we'd end up with really be a centrist? Nor would anything helpful result in the case of a person who tried to accept only half of what liberals and conservatives defend. Instead of being a centrist, such a person would end up only looking confused!

There is a solution to our little problem. Suppose we agree that the true center or mainstream is composed of all those beliefs and positions that happen to be *true*. Hence, if the conservative position is true, then it deserves to be considered the center or mainstream—likewise for the liberal position. But since it's unlikely that we'll get many liberals to acknowledge the truth of conservative positions, and vice versa, the true nature of the evangelical center will continue to elude us. We'll never be able to resolve the content of the evangelical center until we resolve the dispute between evangelical liberals and conservatives.

THE RELIGIOUS RIGHT

The Religious Right and the Moral Majority
During the early 1980s, the terms *the religious right* and *the Moral Majority* were often used interchangeably. But even during its heyday, Jerry Falwell's Moral Majority organization was only one small part of the large army of politically conservative evangelicals—most of whom didn't align themselves with any organized group. Today, of course, the Moral Majority no longer exists as an organization. But the religious right may be stronger and better organized than it has ever been. So is the religious left.

Of course, both "religious right" and "Moral Majority" have been terms of reproach. There has been a concerted effort to get Americans to believe that these terms describe fanatical, irrational extremists who are a threat to basic American values. Something along these lines seems to be the mission of the organization called People for an American Way. This misconception was perpetuated by members of the media, whose own liberal bias has been documented in such sources as the Rothman-Lichter Report. When a powerful media constantly beats their drum about the dreaded religious right and when millions of uninformed people who don't know better believe what they hear, it becomes relatively easy to caricature any conservative opinion as out of step with the American mainstream.

Four Weaknesses of the Religious Right
In spite of misconceptions about the religious right caused by the misrepresentations of many in the information and entertainment industries, four weaknesses of the religious right must be noted.

Christianity and American Civil Religion
America has long had a civil religion that has existed alongside Christianity and that has frequently been confused with it. This American civil religion is often on public display during holidays like the Fourth of July. I don't know that I necessarily have anything against some manifestations of civil religion. I readily confess to getting a lump in my throat and a tear in my eye when I hear Sandi Patti sing the "Star Spangled Banner." But when I travel to Russia, I don't go there to invite Russians to become followers of America's civil religion. I go there to invite them to accept Jesus Christ as personal Savior and Lord. Whatever evangelicals think and do with regard to America's civil religion, they must be careful never to confuse it with Christianity.

Christianity and Capitalism
The second weakness of the religious right is its tendency to equate Christianity and capitalism. Of course, nothing in this last statement should be taken as a criticism of capitalism. But even if we grant that capitalism is superior to its alternatives, Christians should avoid talking and acting as though the two systems are in some way equivalent. Nor does it help when overzealous Christians make exaggerated claims about what

they perceive to be the Bible's teaching about economics.[8]

A corollary of this weakness is the inability of many American Christians to understand the true nature of capitalism, a fact that explains the haste with which they equate capitalism with the quite different economic system presently operating in the U.S. It is wiser, I think, to recognize that the American economic system today is not a capitalist or market system, but is rather an imperfect mixture of limited markets and massive governmental intervention.[9] Of course, from my perspective it would help if the religious left could see this same point. Liberals are quick to note failings of the American economic system, but I believe they are wrong when they blame these faults on capitalism. As I have argued elsewhere, these failings are more often than not the product of the same kinds of governmental interventionism that many politicians want to expand.[10]

Christianity and "Conservative" Politicians

The third weakness of the religious right is the widespread gullibility that leads many conservatives to support people who appear to espouse their principles but who in fact do not hold Christian values at all. This gullibility results whenever Christians allow politicians to "blow in their ears" if the politicians hold the "correct" political views, while allowing them uncritically to get away with questionable activities once in office. Of course, some would counter that other Christians evidence the same kind of gullibility with respect to liberal politicians. The evangelical vote in 1988 clearly helped get George Bush elected to the presidency. Once the election was over, Bush promptly forgot the religious right until the demands of the 1992 campaign made it clear how badly he needed the movement on his side.

Christianity and One-Issue Politics

The fourth weakness of the religious right is its tendency toward one-issue politics. It is not wise to evaluate *everything* through a one-issue lens, as many conservatives do with the issue of abortion. Such reasoning obscures the validity of a candidate's or person's thinking on other issues of equal or perhaps greater value. But at the same time, the realities of current political battles suggest that assorted issues often get consolidated into packages. While exceptions do occur, it is frequently the case that the candidate who satisfies, let us say, the conservative voter on the abortion issue will often be conservative on other major issues as well. Similarly, the politician who takes his or her stand in support of abortion-on-demand will in many cases satisfy liberal voters on a wide range of issues.

The Religious Right Today

The religious right appeared to be in decline during the last years of the 1980s. Scandals involving several nationally prominent televangelists hurt the public's view of Christians. Insufficient attention was paid to the fact that the individuals involved were more closely aligned with the charismatic movement than with evangelicalism. Jerry Falwell's decision to close down the Moral Majority organization seemed to some to be another sign that politically conservative Christians were losing ground.

One important thing to remember about this whole matter is the distinction between organizations and the mass of people who think, act, and vote independent of any organization. There appear to be about fifty million evangelicals in the United States—most of whom are conservative on social issues. Of course, it is impossible to say how many of these millions are informed social activists with the ability to separate fact from fiction in a political campaign.

Viewed from the perspective of late 1992, significant elements of the evangelical right have regained influence within the Republican Party. Pat Robertson, Jerry Falwell, and D. James Kennedy all were prominent during the Republican National Convention. The influence of religious conservatives on the 1992 Republican Platform cannot be ignored. At

various times during the 1992 presidential campaign, George
Bush and Dan Quayle reiterated favorite themes of American
evangelicals, such as family values and choice in education.
Also significant is the increasing activism of millions of evangelicals who see the Democratic Party as a threat to important
social and family values.

THE RELIGIOUS LEFT

The Rise of the Evangelical Left

The sharp divisions among evangelicals over political issues
first became apparent in the 1960s and 1970s—a time that
interestingly coincides with the rise of the new left and various forms of political radicalism. Whatever one makes of this
coincidence, during this period a number of evangelicals published books attacking what the evangelical liberals called an
uncritical alliance between theologically conservative Christians and the political right in the U.S.[11] Some claims in these
books were undoubtedly correct, but many careful students
of the issues were troubled by several weaknesses. For one
thing, the authors seemed totally unfamiliar with the writings
of responsible representatives of the conservative movement
who had disassociated their movement from racists and other
extremists who, the conservatives insisted, were not conservative at all.

In their writings, some evangelical critics of conservatism
tried to poison the well by seeking to link politically conservative Christians with radical extremists.

The evangelical liberals also demonstrated a surprising
unfamiliarity with even the most rudimentary principles of
economic thinking. Moreover, conservatives wondered if the
spokesmen for the evangelical left were not simply replacing the
uncritical alliance with the political right, which they claimed to
find in conservatism, with an equally uncritical alliance with the
left. There was also concern about the left's apparent arrogance

and intolerance toward Christians who held any view of society that differed from their own. It looked very much as though the religious left had given birth to a new kind of separatism—one centered around political convictions and voting habits.

The attacks from the religious left took a more savage turn in the mid-seventies when some equated political conservatism with selfish materialism and a callous indifference to the poor. By this time, it had become a sin, these people suggested, to vote for candidates like Ronald Reagan. On a number of evangelical college and seminary campuses, political conservatism was equated with anti-Christian attitudes.

By the early eighties, a number of evangelicals had moved far beyond traditional forms of political liberalism toward a kind of Marxism being advocated by liberation theologians.[12] In this view, all poverty results from oppression, specifically, an oppression that these far-left extremists associated with the U.S. and capitalism.

Of course, not all the people in the evangelical left supported extremism of this type. This underscores the importance of drawing some distinctions within the evangelical left.

Distinctions Within the Religious Left
Three distinct groups within the evangelical left will be identified. While other groups and individuals have different characteristics, these three are representative.

Evangelicals for Social Action
The driving force in Evangelicals for Social Action (ESA) has been Ronald Sider, a professor of theology at Eastern Baptist Theological Seminary near Philadelphia. Sider, a Mennonite, is a committed Christian with a deep concern for the poor. While Sider is often criticized for being a socialist, he denies the validity of the charge. Lately he has stated that capitalism is the best hope the world's poor have if they are ever to be delivered from poverty.[13]

One is unlikely to find many members of ESA defending a strong national defense or programs like the Strategic Defense Initiative.[14] While such stands may be less significant following the dissolution of the Soviet Union, some critics point out that had America's leaders followed the advice of some in ESA, the dramatic changes that have occurred in the USSR might not have taken place.

ESA exemplifies the moderate evangelical left at the end of the twentieth century. Many in ESA would differ from the typical Democratic platform on one point: the issue of abortion. Most ESA supporters follow Sider's lead in opposing abortion. Of course, as noted in chapter 1, their pro-life stance does not often result in their voting against pro-abortion politicians.

One can find chapters of ESA on most evangelical college and seminary campuses. Other than Ron Sider, probably the best-known evangelical supporter of the ESA program is nationally known lecturer and author Tony Campolo.

The Grand Rapids Movement

A second movement of the evangelical left was formerly identified in terms of its relationship to *The Reformed Journal*, a monthly publication out of Grand Rapids, Michigan, which had close ties to Eerdmans Publishing Company and some faculty members at Calvin College. While there were some exceptions, many of the people whose names used to appear on the masthead of *The Reformed Journal* represented the moderate-left stance we're examining in this section. While *The Reformed Journal* has ceased publication, its editorial perspective and many of the same people are now associated with a different monthly called *Perspectives*.

While the Grand Rapids movement (for want of a better name) is somewhat less predictable than other segments of the evangelical left, its representatives would strongly disagree with the views of fundamentalists, theonomists, pentecostals, charismatics, capitalists, and Republicans (at least, conservative

Republicans). They clearly don't like the views of Ronald Reagan, Pat Robertson, Jerry Falwell, Francis Schaeffer, Phyllis Schlaffley, or Rush Limbaugh. This has led one critic to quip that other than themselves, Mother Teresa, and whoever the Democratic presidential candidate may be, it is difficult to know who they do like. All in all, what one tends to get from the Grand Rapids group is the viewpoint of liberal Democrats, even though in some cases the spokespeople may be liberal Republicans.

The Radical Religious Left
Earlier, the reader will remember, I did attack the radical religious right, a haven for quacks, weirdos, and the intensely uninformed. Because the radical right is so well known, it was unnecessary to go into much detail on its aberrant beliefs and behavior. But the radical religious left is not nearly so well known. Hence, attention to its peculiarities seems justified. To eliminate the possible charge that I am exaggerating, I will quote from a 1988 article that appeared in the journal *Transformation*, published by Evangelicals for Social Action. The article was written by Bernard Adeney, a professor at New College, a small Christian college in Berkeley, California.

Alluding to the United States, Dr. Adeney claimed that "the wealthiest nation with the most Christians is spending *trillions* of dollars on threats to destroy the earth."[15] Let me suggest that the reader pause, reread the last sentence several times, and reflect a moment. Adeney goes on to state that he rejects the claim that the United States' real intent in spending money on national defence is "to hold back world-wide tyranny." Rather, he contends, the real purpose is "to achieve world dominance . . . to extend U.S. power and influence."[16]

To someone unfamiliar with the rhetoric of the far left, the initial result of an encounter with such claims is likely to be sheer astonishment. We are accustomed to irrational conspiracy theories and paranoia from representatives of the far right. We can readily understand how difficult it must be to reason with anyone suffering from delusions. If similar problems afflict the people on the far left, can there be much hope for a rational discussion of the issues, even if the extremist is a Christian? Not surprisingly, Adeney offers no evidence to support his contention; it springs entirely from his imagination. As Dean Curry, professor of government at Messiah College, points out, Adeney's claim that "the United States [spends] monies on military hardware in order to threaten the destruction of the world . . . has itself no basis in fact. Emotive language and sloganeering . . . is no substitute for a reasoned analysis of the moral dimensions of deterrence."[17] Nor does Adeney reveal any ability to understand the real threats the Soviet military posed in the world before the recent dramatic changes in the Soviet Union. As I said before, some have pointed out that those changes might never have occurred if the U.S. had followed the political agenda of the evangelical left.

One person and organization that comes to mind when thinking of the radical religious left is Jim Wallis and his monthly magazine, *Sojourners*. Many movements that start out radical tend to become more moderate with the passing of time. This has not been true of *Sojourners*. The only thing that some people have seen weakening over the years has been the magazine's commitment to evangelical theology and a strong emphasis on the human need for repentance from personal sin and reliance on the atoning work of Christ for personal salvation. *Sojourners* has seemed more interested in collective guilt resulting from what it sees as American-capitalist oppression of the poor and a "salvation" of the oppressed from social evils, such as racism, sexism, militarism, and homophobia.

Richard John Neuhaus is a sober and judicious commentator on contemporary religion and society. In spite of his impeccable credentials as a former representative of the political left, Neuhaus warns that *Sojourners* "represents a politically extreme, profoundly self-righteous, and virulently anti-intellectual version of [what Jim Wallis calls] 'biblical politics.'"[18]

One telling revelation of the true nature of the religious far left has come from the typewriter of one of its early founders, evangelical theologian Clark Pinnock. Pinnock was not only present at the birth of what became the Sojourners movement, he also served on the magazine's editorial board for several years.

Pinnock describes his support for the radical left in those early years as the result of a kind of conversion. In 1970, he explained, his "political thinking underwent a paradigm shift—a total transformation." He found himself looking at society from the perspective we now call the new left. He came to believe that the Bible obliged him to reject anything connected with democratic capitalism. "It was," he explained, "a new political-theological world to move in and it produced a heady experience which intoxicated me and many others. It led me personally to sympathy and support for the Marxist movements of the world."[19]

After eight years in the radical movement, Pinnock felt new opinions stirring within him. As he wrote, "Gradually, I began to reassess my position and my alienation from North America began to fade, replaced by a certain critical appreciation of democratic capitalism that I had had before 1970."[20]

Pinnock tells of a time when someone asked him if he realized how much Marxism there was within the pages of *Sojourners*, when he was still serving as its editor. Up to that point it had not occurred to him that so much of what the magazine and the movement held was advocating a Marxist worldview. Pinnock describes the attraction that socialism had for him and others in the movement. He thought that socialism was "a grand vision of a just and humane order which distributed its resources fairly and equitably among all its people according to their need. . . . Without equating the two, it was so easy for me to associate in my mind the socialist utopia and the promised kingdom of

God. . . . We admired what we thought was happening in the new China under Mao, and we hoped that the Viet Cong would win out against American forces."[21]

What finally brought Pinnock to his senses? He explained,

It now struck me as somewhat ridiculous to overlook those positive features of North American life which had incidentally made it possible for radicals like me to express and live out our concerns. How could I have had such deep contempt for a culture which surely stands as a beacon of hope in this suffering world? How ironic to call for "liberation" in the very place there is probably more of it than anywhere else in the world, and to be sympathetic toward those societies where neither liberty nor justice is in good supply. It began to dawn on me that if one was looking for Babylon in this present world, one might rather look toward the threat of totalitarian government.[22]

Pinnock changed his mind, both about the U.S. and communism. "What really endangers liberty and justice in our world," he wrote, "is not a flawed America, but that political monism, whether of the fascist right or the communist left, which declares itself to be absolute and answers to no transcendent value."[23]

Pinnock also changed his mind about democratic capitalism. "Far from being the enemy of the poor," he wrote, capitalism "now seems to me to offer both liberty and prosperity in abundance and to deserve our cautious support. Socialism, on the other hand, has a dismal record of providing neither."[24]

Pinnock's candid confession of how he was seduced into accepting the worldview of the secular new left and the evangelical radicals is a powerful exposé of the workings of the radical mind. It confirms the account of the religious far left presented in this chapter. The tragedy is that every year large numbers of Christian young people who know nothing about Pinnock's pilgrimage are seduced through similar arguments offered by professors on college campuses. The religious far left keeps rolling along, oblivious to the powerful economic and philosophic case that has been mustered against it.

Jim Wallis and others in the religious far left claim to be part of an ideologically pure, nonpolitical movement that has supposedly arisen from a fresh reading of the Bible. But, their critics point out, the far-left extremists have not been faithful to the social message of the Bible. They have simply surrendered to the prevailing ideology of the political far left and have read the content of *that* message into God's Word.

Three Weaknesses of the Religious Left
Earlier in this chapter, I identified four weaknesses of the religious right. In this section, I will discuss three weaknesses of the religious left. Before I do that, however, I want to mention two additional weaknesses that used to characterize the religious left but have become largely irrelevant since the collapse of communism in the former Soviet Union. First, when the Soviet Union was still a political entity, the religious left in the U.S. followed the lead of the secular left in espousing the doctrine of moral equivalence. As Dean Curry wrote, this was the belief "that the United States and the Soviet Union [were] two similar kinds of nations. Both . . . systems [were] repressive and both of their foreign policies [were] characterized by brutality as they [sought] to exploit and dominate others. In short, in terms of their motivations and their actions, the conclusion [was] drawn that both nations are morally equivalent."[25] On this view of things, there were no moral differences between the United States and the Soviet Union. Under no conditions could the U.S. be seen as morally superior to the old Soviet Union. For someone who thought this way, it could not possibly make a bit of difference which nation might win or lose the cold war.

Christian Americans could not possibly support anything the U.S. might do to deter aggression. The world could not possibly be worse off if the U.S. lost; so people of this persuasion thought.

Of course, now that the Soviet Union has dissolved and the leaders of the new Russia have opened the files of their military and secret police, anyone who cares to look can find all the evidence needed to disprove the doctrine of moral equivalence. Along with these revelations come ample expressions of shame at what previous leaders of the old USSR did to innocent Soviet citizens as well as to innocent people from other nations. Some members of the religious left in the U.S. would like their former defense of moral equivalence to be forgotten.

Another former weakness of the religious left that, for the moment at least, is moot was the zealous way many representatives of the movement kept calling on the U.S. to disarm itself unilaterally, without any regard for reciprocal acts on the part of the Soviet Union. Ronald Sider was an outspoken advocate for this view in the early 1980s. Sider realized that such action would in all likelihood be followed by an occupation of the U.S. by the Red Army and such allies as Cuba and East Germany. Sider's recommendation to Christians during such an occupation was passive resistance along the lines of Ghandi.

It apparently did not occur to members of the religious left that a policy they recommended because it would supposedly lessen tension and danger in the world would result instead in enormous injustice and loss of life. Now that the peoples of Russia, the Ukraine, and other former republics of the USSR have repudiated the communist system, there may be merit in reflecting on how different the world would be today if the U.S. had followed the advice of the religious left. These former problems need no further discussion in the light of new world conditions, but three weaknesses of the religious left must still be noted.

The Religious Left and the Difference Between Means and Ends

The word *ends* refers, of course, to the goals or objectives that people seek to realize. I have argued for years that there is little real difference between the ends desired by liberal and conservative Christians. Both groups want to end or at least minimize *injustice.* The debate turns, however, on what each group means by *justice* and the means (policies) they think will best accomplish that end.[26]

Both groups are opposed to racism. Both want to see the poor of the world helped and uplifted. The persistent suggestion that conservatives are less caring and compassionate than liberals is outrageous. The tension between liberals and conservatives would be lessened considerably if liberals would concede that conservatives share similar ends but disagree about the best means to achieve those goals.

The Religious Left and Their Preferred Means

Few Christians have the time or opportunity to do serious research on any technical subject, let alone the complex issues encountered in social theory. Christians who work in the academic world are supposed to be an exception to this, however. Economists and social theorists have produced an enormous amount of literature over the past fifteen years that points to serious defects in the means or policies that American liberals have recommended to "solve" this or that social problem. After almost thirty years of welfare programs in the United States, a mountain of data shows how useless or harmful most of these programs have been.[27] For any Christian familiar with this enormous body of literature, it is embarrassing to observe the silence on the part of many in the religious left. Many continue to proclaim the old dogmas (or at least never acknowledge their errors), oblivious to the fact that they are defending hopeless proposals. A pervasive streak of utopianism runs through much liberal rhetoric. Many seem convinced that, for every social problem, some governmental program can solve that problem. But most of the time, any new programs they recommend are simply variations on programs that have been tried and have failed.

Now there are some refreshing exceptions. Ronald Sider, for example, appears to have been listening to some arguments of conservative social theorists. This could help explain why some of the things Sider says today differ considerably from claims he made a decade ago.

It is not my intention to suggest that conservative arguments are always superior to liberal arguments. My complaint concerns the failure of so many religious liberals to engage those arguments. I applaud those, like Sider, who are doing so.

The Religious Left and Notions of Peace and Justice

A friend told me recently that he had been at a gathering of evangelicals who had been asked to stand, identify themselves, and name the organization they represented. After a number of people had done so, it was the turn of a person who worked for a left-of-center evangelical organization. After giving his name and identifying his organization, he added with an air of smug satisfaction, "I am a peace and justice Christian!" His implication was impossible to miss. In his exalted view of himself, he was the *only* Christian in the room working for peace and justice.

I share this incident not to comment on the arrogance and sense of moral superiority this person exuded, but to introduce the importance of the twin notions of peace and justice for members of the religious left. I repudiate totally any suggestion that the religious left has a monopoly on the vitally important concepts of peace and justice. Moreover, I believe any careful analysis of the terms will reveal some serious problems in the way the religious left handles these notions.

Consider, for example, the left's distortion of the biblical term *shalom* (peace). The left misuses *shalom* to justify a form of pacifism that would have allowed countless tyrants, from Hitler to Stalin to those in the present day, the opportunity to impose their ruthless power on helpless people. Allowing the enemies of peace and justice such a free hand is hardly the sort of thing that peace and justice Christians should be doing.

But, as Dean Curry notes, the religious left also misuses *shalom* "to legitimate political agendas that are more often than not ideologically leftist."[28] Such actions ignore the fact that there are three types of peace in the Bible. The first is peace with God. The second is peace with oneself. And finally there is the important matter of achieving peace among human beings. The first two kinds of peace are available only to believers in Christ. Biblically, the third type (peace among humans) is never equated with pacifism. It refers instead to the absence of conflict. The religious left tends to ignore how the absence of conflict in the real world is, more often than not, a consequence of non-aggressor nations being strong enough to deter aggression, both against themselves and against weaker nations.

Peace and justice Christians also overlook the fact that the biblical concept of *shalom* contains nuances not found in the English word *peace*, such as the ideas of completeness and wholeness. This leads Dean Curry to say that *shalom* "is a gift of God, brought about, not through the work of man's hands, but by God. The peace of *shalom* is an eschatalogical peace which awaits the consummation of history itself."[29] Hence, biblical *shalom* is not simply the absence of war; therefore, it cannot be tied in any essential way to pacifism. Prudent and realistic Christians will easily see that the religious left's pursuit of "peace" on its terms will only make the world a more dangerous place for everyone. Real peace in the real world is the last thing the policies of peace and justice Christians will realize.

Nor does the religious left's notion of justice fare any better. Building on the work of several published studies,[30] Dean Curry points out that the Bible never uses the word *justice* "in the modern sense of social justice, which the Left take to mean a situation in which the state uses its coercive powers to redistribute society's holdings to assure an equal outcome."[31] Biblical uses of *justice* refer to righteousness or virtue. For example, when the Bible reports that Noah was a just man, it does not necessarily mean that he would have voted for liberal social programs. It means that he was a virtuous, righteous man. In a smaller number of cases, the Bible uses *justice* in the sense of treating people fairly in particular situations involving business transactions or courtroom decisions.

All of this leads Curry to this conclusion:

> The Bible states that God's expectation is that the righteous person—the just person—cares about the poor and oppressed. The Bible does not teach, however, that the poor and oppressed are that way because others are rich. Nor does the Bible teach that the way to help the poor and oppressed is to support revolutionary liberation movements, socialist economics, and Marxist politics. Yet, this is often the agenda of "peace and justice" Christians.[32]

While few Christians would disagree with our need to be concerned with issues of peace and justice, greater care should be given to how we unpack the meaning of these terms. And greater wisdom should be shown in the means we select to reach these ends. In the meantime, there is no reason to accept the claim that the religious left has a monopoly on the issues of peace and justice.

The Religious Left Today

Some segments of the extreme left seem to be showing signs of decline. The Sojourners community in Washington, D.C., has split several times and barely survives, while the number of subscribers to the movement's magazine is dropping. Jim Wallis travels around the country with a popular Christian musician trying to renew interest in his message.

But if I were a member of the moderate religious left today, I'd feel optimistic about the future. Members of the religious left exercise a strong influence over many evangelical colleges, institutions, organizations, and publications. The future does look bright for the moderate religious left.

IS THERE ANY HOPE FOR EASING THE POLITICAL DIVISION WITHIN THE CHURCH?

Large numbers of Bible-believing Christians are clearly polarized over the issues covered in this chapter. I can imagine many readers thinking that after covering all this controversy, I will somehow pull a rabbit out of the hat and describe ways to end all this bitter turmoil. Unfortunately, there is no one presently alive on planet earth who can do *that*. I can offer several observations and suggestions that may provide help for the reader.

First, it would be a mistake to think that increasing Christian unity requires that Christians stop disagreeing with each other. Just because people disagree doesn't mean they cannot work together in love. If easing the present tension in the church meant that conservatives must become liberals or vice versa, prospects for greater unity would be pretty bleak. Anyone who seriously advances something like this as the grounds for ending Christian disunity just isn't being realistic.

The fact that we disagree is not what is causing tension within the church; the *way* we disagree is the source of most of our problems. If I'm a conservative and some other person is a liberal, that person does not have to renounce his views in order for us to be friends. I have many friends within the camp of the religious left. So, relinquishing the beliefs that divide us is not a necessary condition for loving fellowship and cooperation in the cause of the gospel.

All of us—and I include myself here—need to pay more

attention to our attitudes toward believers with whom we disagree. Some Christian conservatives demonstrate more love and understanding for unsaved people in other countries than they offer to brothers and sisters in the evangelical left. Members of the religious left don't help the situation when they exhibit an air of smugness and moral superiority and dismiss any who disagree with them as selfish materialists who lack compassion for the poor.

Less pride and more self-honesty wouldn't hurt, either. All of us are sinful creatures, and one persistent sign of that is our reluctance to admit our past mistakes. Perhaps a bit more self-honesty would lead us to admit that some of our convictions on these issues don't come from God's Word after all but are things we've picked up from our surrounding culture and are now reading into Scripture.

Moderates in both the religious right and left also need to pay more attention to some common interests. Most of us are committed to defending the cause of unborn babies. All of us, I think, want to help the poor and oppressed people around the world. We are concerned about peace and justice. Seldom do we disagree over ends. People who share a common faith in Jesus Christ, who profess to get their marching orders from the same Bible, and who agree about so many common social ends ought to be closer than in fact we are.

Here and there, in little meetings that few people know or seem to care about, small numbers of people from the religious right and left are sitting down, breaking bread together, and with love and respect exploring ways to bridge the gaps that separate them. Whether these little groups will grow in size and whether the separating gaps will diminish is something still hidden in the mist of the future. But it is something we can work toward.

Chapter Eight

THE CONTROVERSY OVER CHRISTIAN RECONSTRUCTIONISTS: ARE THEY DANGEROUS?

❖

Some widely read Christian authors have claimed recently that there are some dangerous characters running around the church. According to one critic, these people profess to be Christians and at the same time are guilty of ignoring heaven. To make things even worse, other critics have charged that this same group of people has made public its opposition to democracy. It has even been charged that these individuals are anti-Semitic and also guilty of laying the groundwork for a new kind of Jewish holocaust.

Who could these people possibly be? Could they be some strange breed of Christian Nazi? Are they possibly an offshoot of the Ku Klux Klan?

Before I incite some kind of public lynching, perhaps I had better quit noting such extreme rhetoric. The subject of this chapter is the very group I've just described. The incredible allegations I've noted have indeed been hurled at "Christian reconstructionists." Obviously, if such charges were true, we would be dealing with some of the most dangerous people in the United States.

Why would a Christian level such charges at another

believer? That is part of the interesting story we'll be uncovering as we seek to answer the question, *Are the Christian reconstructionists dangerous?*

THE VALUE OF THIS STUDY

Discovering the truth about Christian reconstructionism is only one of the reasons I've included this chapter. Large numbers of Christians want to know who these people are and if they really hold the beliefs that have been attributed to them. But I must also acknowledge that millions have never heard the word *reconstructionist* or the related term, *theonomist*. Since many in this second group may find it hard to care about this subject, it will help to point out other reasons why the material in this chapter is important to any Christian reader.

For one thing, reconstructionists raise significant questions about the relationship between the Old Testament (OT) law and the New Testament (NT). Christians recognize that the Jewish system of animal sacrifice in the OT has been abolished—this is clear in the Epistle to the Hebrews. But what about the Ten Commandments? Surely the NT teaches the abiding relevance and importance of the Mosaic law, even if obeying it cannot produce salvation. The reader may have wondered what he or she should make of the abundance of other laws and prescriptions that fill the pages of the Pentateuch.

The position we'll be examining in this chapter challenges believers of all stripes to think about these other OT laws because, it insists, those laws are still binding on Christians (unless explicitly rescinded in the NT). Advocates of the theonomic position maintain that the OT laws will form the legal framework of Christ's kingdom on earth. So, the ideas we'll be looking at in this chapter raise a challenging question about how Christians should understand the relationship between OT law and NT teaching.

But this chapter is important for another reason: It helps

answer questions raised in other chapters in this book. Chapter 10 will introduce the dispute between *premillennialists* and *amillennialists*. This chapter will preview some of that debate by focusing on the view held by yet another group of Christians: *postmillennialists*.

Finally, this chapter will also fill in some gaps left over from the last chapter where we discussed the controversy over Christian involvement in politics. Once Christians recognize the urgency of becoming politically active, they will find the need for information about the major positions that are held by other evangelical believers. This chapter will alert them to one of those groups. I doubt that anyone would ever confuse a member of the evangelical left with the people or positions we'll look at in this chapter. But are these people and positions synonymous with the religious right, which we studied in the last chapter? Would Jerry Falwell be part of this group? If not, where does this group fit in relation to people like him?

Even if we discover that many of the views we examine are mistaken, we can learn some things by recognizing where some godly people who set out to be faithful to God's Word have come to positions with which we disagree.

Though some people view Christian reconstructionists as allegedly dangerous, as I'll explain shortly, a major part of the confusion one encounters in this matter is due to a sloppy use of the reconstructionist name. So the first step we'll take in dealing with this particular "great divide" is to clarify the meaning of the word *reconstructionism* and distinguish it from the real targets of the above-mentioned criticisms, a smaller group of Christians who subscribe to a theological position known as "theonomy."

WHAT IS CHRISTIAN RECONSTRUCTIONISM?

The best way to develop an answer to the question, "What is Christian reconstructionism?" is by a little diagram that distinguishes three kinds of Christian social activists. By "social activists" I simply mean people who believe their Christian faith obliges them to change things in society that they believe are not only harmful to human beings, but incompatible with what God teaches in His Word. It is also important to point out that most Christian social activists seem to share the same goals or objectives. They are concerned to help people who are poor, oppressed, or hurting in some way. Where Christian social activists seem to disagree is in the means they select to reach their goals. This diagram distinguishes these three major groups:

EVANGELICAL SOCIAL ACTIVISTS

| The Evangelical Left | Conservatives Who Are Not Reconstructionists | Reconstructionists |

These three groups are all committed to influencing their society in ways that reflect their understanding of God's Word. One major point to notice on the diagram is that an evangelical Christian can be politically and socially conservative (in contrast to the evangelical left, which generally takes a liberal stance) without also being a reconstructionist.

Since I discussed the other two groups of social activists in chapter 7, they will disappear from sight during the rest of this chapter. One goal of this chapter is to clarify the nature of reconstructionism as a Christian way of thinking about society and politics. Unpacking the meaning of one word—*dominion*—will move us closer to that goal.

Dominion in Genesis 1:26—The Cultural Mandate
The concept of dominion is crucial to any reconstructionist's understanding of personal Christian duty in God's world. The idea of dominion harks back to God's creation mandate in Genesis 1:26—"Then God said, 'Let us make man in our image, in our likeness, and let them rule over the fish of the sea and the birds of the air, over the livestock, over all the earth, and over all the crea-

tures that move along the ground.'" In this and following verses, it becomes clear that God gave humans dominion over this earth.

An important corollary of this cultural mandate is that *the Bible applies to every area of life*. All reconstructionists believe in dominion, in some sense. Where they differ is in the specific way this dominion should be worked out. The reconstructionist believes that Christians who allow Satan and his followers to exercise dominion over this world are betraying God and His cultural mandate. It is the Christian's duty to resist the devil, to resist evil, including evil people and evil institutions. It is our duty to seek to bring all human society under the dominion of God's Holy Word. This is what Christian reconstructionists believe. This is an appropriate time for the reader to pause and reflect on where he or she stands with regard to the idea of dominion.

A reconstructionist is, in the broadest sense of the term, simply a Christian who believes it is his or her responsibility to challenge the anti-Christian character of society and culture. The reconstructionist sees it as an obligation to seek to change society in ways that will bring it into conformity with the teaching of Scripture. It is important to note that a reconstructionist (in this broad sense of the word) need *not* believe that God's model for society is necessarily found in the civil code of the Pentateuch, the first five books of the Bible.[1] This last view, however, is central to the beliefs of people who call themselves theonomists.

Reconstructionists believe American society is in desperate need of reconstruction: Our nation's leaders have failed us, they say, leading us down the path to policies that are self-destructive and unbiblical. Reconstructionists believe that the only hope for our nation is to bring it into closer alignment with patterns that God has revealed in His Word.

WHAT IS A THEONOMIST?

The best approach to answering the question, "What is a theonomist?" begins with a part of our first diagram and then builds on it. The diagram on page 156 illustrated how reconstructionists differ from other Christian social activists. This second diagram indicates how theonomists are related to Christian reconstructionism in general and how they differ from advocates of reconstructionism who reject theonomy.

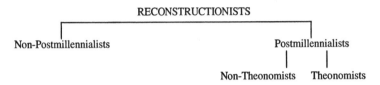

Notice three initial points indicated in the diagram. (1) If someone is a theonomist, then that person accepts a position on the end times called postmillennialism. (2) Many reconstructionists reject postmillennialism. (3) And to make things even more complicated, some postmillennial reconstructionists are not theonomists. How do we unpack all this theological baggage?

UNDERSTANDING THE VARIOUS "MILLENNIAL" VIEWPOINTS

Now I know that this seems complicated. It is! And it's easy to get confused as to who is and who is not a theonomist. But stick with me. I'll try to eliminate some of this confusion, beginning by explaining the various views of the millennium, for example, what *postmillennialism* is. But that will require that I also explain what the millennium is and how postmillennialism differs from two other positions known as *premillennialism* and *amillennialism.*

Premillennialists
The word *millennium* refers to the period of one thousand years mentioned in Revelation 20:1-10. People who call themselves premillennialists interpret that passage in a more literal sense

than others. They believe, therefore, that Christ will actually rule this planet for a thousand years sometime in the future. What makes a person a premillennialist is the additional belief that Christ's Second Coming will occur *before* the establishment of the earthly millennial kingdom.[2]

Amillennialists

Many Christians hold to the position known as amillennialism, which interprets the thousand years of Revelation 20 in a figurative way. For an amillennialist, there will be no literal thousand-year reign of Christ on earth. When this age ends, there will be only one return of Christ to earth, to be followed immediately by the final judgment where God will forever separate believers from unbelievers.[3]

Postmillennialists

Postmillennialists believe that Christ's Second Coming will occur *after* the millennium.[4] There is no need, postmillennialists believe, to take the number 1000 literally. However long the period of time may prove to be, the point is that God will use His church to prepare the world for Christ's eventual return.

Postmillennialists anticipate a time in which the church's influence will continue to grow as millions of people are evangelized and brought to faith. Evangelical postmillennialists do not believe the church will "bring in the kingdom." That is God's work. Nor do evangelical postmillennialists believe in the inherent goodness of human beings. They do not teach that the world will get better and better in the sense taught by religious modernists earlier in this century.

On the contrary, they have unbounded confidence in the power *of God* to convert the unsaved and through His Spirit to bring the growing number of converted to live as Christians ought to live, thus changing the character of their homes, communities, and eventually their nations. It is their optimism about the effect that God's Word and God's Spirit can have upon the world that grounds their social activism. They refuse to abandon the world to Satan. To do so, they believe, would constitute a betrayal of their Christian responsibility.

Glancing back at the diagram on page 158, we find that *some* reconstructionists are postmillennialists and thus believe that their social activism will help fulfill the eschatalogical plan that they find in Scripture. But there are plenty of reconstructionists who are not postmillennialists.[5] And, as mentioned earlier, there are also some postmillennial reconstructionists who are not theonomists![6]

THEONOMISTS AND THE PENTATEUCH'S CIVIL CODE

What, then, is a theonomist? So far we have learned that a theonomist is a postmillennial reconstructionist. But this must be amplified since others who fit this description are not theonomists. And so we must go a step further and define a theonomist as a postmillennial reconstructionist *who believes that God's model for reconstructed human society is found in the entire Bible, both Old and New Testaments, including the civil code of the Pentateuch.*

All reconstructionists attempt to give direction and content to what it means to take dominion. Theonomy is only one specific way of identifying this content. A theonomist, then, is a special kind of reconstructionist, one who believes in the abiding validity of the Mosaic law as part of God's model for human society.

All theonomists, therefore, are reconstructionists, but not all reconstructionists are theonomists. For example, television minister, Dr. D. James Kennedy identifies himself as a reconstructionist; but Kennedy clearly separates himself from the theonomist movement.

Gary DeMar, a theonomist associated with the organization American Vision in Atlanta, states that theonomists "believe that the Word of God, that is, '*all* Scripture,' should be applied to *all* areas of life. With such faithful application, [theonomists] expect that God will bless the efforts of His people in both 'this age' and in the 'age to come' (Mark 10:29-31)."[7]

The work of dominion is God's work, is inseparable from evangelism and conversion, cannot be effected through any exclusively political process, and will take a *very* long time. As Greg Bahnsen and Kenneth Gentry explain,

> Post-millennialism . . . expects the gradual, develop-mental expansion of the kingdom of God in time and on earth. This expansion will proceed by means of the full-orbed ministry of the Word, fervent and believing prayer, and the consecrated labors of His Spirit-filled people, all directed and blessed by the ever-present Christ, Who is now at the right hand of God ruling and reigning over the earth.[8]

Moreover, they continue, postmillennialism looks forward to a time in the history of the earth "in which the very gospel already operative in the world will have won the victory throughout the earth in fulfillment of the Great Commission. During that time," Bahnsen and Gentry argue, "the overwhelming majority of men and nations will be Christianized, righteousness will abound, wars will cease, and prosperity and safety will flourish. After an extended period of gospel prosperity, earth history will be drawn to a close by the personal, visible, bodily return of Jesus Christ (accompanied by a literal resurrection and a general judgment) to introduce His blood-bought people into the consummative and eternal form of the kingdom, and so shall we ever be with the Lord."[9]

WHO ARE THE THEONOMISTS?

It is now time for a third diagram to help answer the question, "Who are the theonomists?"

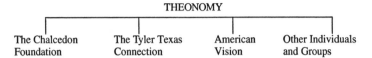

The acknowledged founder of theonomy is Rousas Rush-doony, the author of many books and head of the Chalcedon Foundation, located in central California. What I call "the Tyler Texas Connection" is a collection of organizations and publications that have some connection to Dr. Gary North. North is the moving force behind a seemingly endless stream of books and newsletters that flow from his Institute for Christian Economics in Tyler and his Dominion Press in Fort Worth, Texas. Gary DeMar of American Vision in Atlanta focuses on church conferences that educate laypeople and pastors on various issues. DeMar has also published widely, including several books jointly issued by American Vision and some of North's publishing enterprises.

Many other individuals and groups represent the theonomist cause. I will mention only two more prominent ones: Greg Bahnsen, now living in Southern California, is the author of what many regard as the most influential theonomist book, *Theonomy in Christian Ethics*.[10] David Chilton, also located in Southern California, is another widely published theonomist author.

I began this chapter by asking, *Are the Christian recon-structionists dangerous?* I pointed out, however, that the real targets of the criticisms we'll be noticing are not reconstructionists per se but a subgroup of reconstructionism known as theonomists. We have now examined several careful distinctions between the two groups so as to avoid confusion. I have explained the major features of theonomy and identified the major representatives of the movement,. namely, Rousas Rushdoony, Gary North, Gary DeMar, Greg Bahnsen, David Chilton. The names of scores of others are familiar to students of the movement. It is these gentlemen and the theonomist movement they represent that are alleged to be so dangerous. This is the movement and the people who are accused of being enemies of democracy, anti-Semites, and extremists guilty of placing the material world ahead of heaven. With these issues now clarified, we can turn our attention to the specific charges against this movement and answer the question of whether *theonomy* is a dangerous movement.

Are Theonomists Guilty of Ignoring Heaven?

This is precisely the charge that Dave Hunt has leveled against theonomists in his book *Whatever Happened to Heaven?* Hunt accuses theonomists of succumbing to the belief that they can transform human society for the better, a belief Hunt labels unbiblical. Hunt accuses them of "an unbiblical earthly mindedness which is contrary to that which Christ encouraged and which characterized the early church."[11]

According to Hunt, the Christian's hope "is not in taking over this world but in being taken to heaven by our Lord, to be married to Him in glory and then to return with Him as part of the armies of heaven to rescue Israel, destroy His enemies, and participate in His millennial reign." Theonomists, Hunt claims, are yielding to the temptation "to be more at home in this world than they should be."[12]

Earlier, we read where theonomists Bahnsen and Gentry believe that God's kingdom "will proceed by means of the full-orbed ministry of the Word, fervent and believing prayer, and the consecrated labors of His spirit-filled people." Do their words sound like they come from people whose priorities are worldly rather than God-centered? Recall the priority they give to the work of evangelism. Keeping in mind that their postmillennial view of things may be wrong (I have already indicated my own disagreement with them), their view of the end times is one in which the preaching of the gospel and the subsequent salvation of millions will lay the foundation for a new kind of social order. In this new millennium the huge increase in the number of regenerated and sanctified people in the world will result in nations actually wanting their civil laws to mirror the laws of God; or so they think. There seems to be a tremendous disparity between the way theonomists describe their mission and the way some critics characterize their beliefs.[13]

One final question: What is wrong with any Christian being concerned enough about evils in society to want to challenge them and change them? Does such an attitude betray a callous disregard for heaven? Some believe pre-tribulationism places human history on a one-way track leading to the horrible devastation of the tribulation period. Since this will result in the inevitable destruction of anything that is good and worthwhile humanly speaking, it is a waste of the Christian's time and energy to attempt to change anything for the better. Therefore, Christians should forget their culture and society and concentrate on only one thing: getting themselves and others ready for the rapture.[14]

Just because a Christian believes he has an obligation to resist evil in society, it hardly follows that this person has forgotten heaven or become entangled in worldly things. It is a misrepresentation of what evangelical social activists stand for to say, as Hunt has been quoted, that they exhibit "an unbiblical earthly mindedness which is contrary to that which Christ encouraged and which characterized the early church." The unbiblical view, many would argue, is the one that would have all Christians sit by passively while our government, our schools, the media, and other social and cultural institutions fall increasingly under the control of individuals who are opposed to God's revealed will.

As for Hunt's charge that Christian social activists are trying to "take over this world," all that is necessary to counter this claim is to go back to the earlier pages of this chapter and read how Bahnsen and Gentry explain the meaning of postmillennialism. It does not take a postmillennialist to see that their account of the central role that evangelism and Christian obedience to the Word of God must play in the transformation of society is miles removed from the repeated distortions that appear throughout Hunt's book.

If the first respect in which theonomists are supposedly dangerous is because they are guilty of ignoring heaven, I judge that they are innocent. What strikes me as the far more serious issue in all this is how and why Dave Hunt could so badly misunderstand the views of the theonomists.

Are Theonomists Guilty of Anti-Semitism?

This accusation first came to my attention while I was browsing through a Christian bookstore and noticed a copy of a Hal Lindsey book *The Road to Holocaust*. As we all know, few words can incite greater emotions than *holocaust* and *anti-Semitism*. Without reading very far in the book, the reader will realize that Lindsey is accusing some Christians of a Nazi-like anti-Semitism that would inevitably lead them to support behavior that might well produce another Jewish holocaust.

Here is how Lindsey introduced his thesis:

> The purpose of [*The Road to Holocaust*] is to warn about a rapidly expanding new movement in the Church that is subtly introducing the same old errors that eventually but inevitably led to centuries of atrocities against the Jews and culminated with the Holocaust of the Third Reich. I do not believe that the leaders of this new movement are consciously anti-Semitic—their historical predecessors were not either. But just as their historical counterparts did, they are setting up a philosophical system that will result in anti-Semitism.[15]

These are obviously serious charges. It is therefore important that we see what arguments, if any, Lindsey offers in support of his claims.

According to this view, *any* Christian who is not a premillennialist (i.e., amillennialists and postmillennialists) is "guilty of creating a climate of thought wherein the Jew is viewed as an obstinate and rebellious pretender to the covenants and promises that are now exclusively owned by the Church. Since in this view the Jew has no more special purpose in God's plan as a national people, [such people] see no reason for [Jews] to exist as a distinct people or as a modern state."[16]

Postmillennialists and amillennialists do believe, for the most part, that there is no future place in God's plan for the nation of Israel. They believe that the Church is composed of all believers of all time and hence includes not only John, Peter and Paul, but also Abraham, Moses and David. As such, the church of the living God is the true Israel and has *always* been the real object of God's promises and covenants.

As Paul states in Romans 2:28-29, being a true Jew is more than an outward or physical matter. It is a matter of what has happened in a person's heart. In Galatians 3:29, Paul wrote, "If you belong to Christ, then you are Abraham's seed, and heirs according to the promise" that God made to Abraham. Consequently, Paul had no problem in identifying the church as the Israel of God (Galatians 6:16). Lindsey's claim, which twists a long-held position into an emotively described view that Jews are "obstinate and rebellious pretenders," is the product of Lindsey's own imagination. His language cannot help but incite people's feelings at the same time that it diverts attention away from a serious study of what the Bible teaches.

Lindsey's disregard for the facts becomes most obvious when he claims that the people he's attacking see *no reason* for Jews "to exist as a distinct people or as a modern state." This confuses those anti-Israeli Arab states that do hold the views he describes with non-premillennial Christians who do not. Such reasoning is badly flawed. For example, I do not believe that the Bible teaches there is a special place in God's end-time plans for the nation of Israel. But I support strongly the right of Jews to exist in peace as a nation. I hold this belief in the same way that I believe the nation of Kuwait has a right to exist free from aggression from a nation like Iraq.

I do not believe the Bible teaches there is any special place in God's prophetic plans for Brazil. But it hardly follows that I or anyone else could reasonably infer that Brazil has no right to exist or that the citizens of Brazil can become fair game for any aggressor nation. The absence of any nation-state in God's prophetic plan has nothing to do with the right of that nation to exist or the right of its citizens to life, liberty, and the pursuit of happiness.

It would be nice if we could excuse Lindsey's exercise in bad logic as a slip of some kind. But we must remember that this fallacious reasoning constitutes his only ground for his charge that theonomists are anti-Semites who are aiding and abetting evil men plotting another holocaust. If the charge were not so monstrous, we could simply dismiss it as theological baloney. But it slanders many good, innocent, and decent people.

Are theonomists (and other non-premillennialists) guilty, therefore, of anti-Semitism, thereby fostering support for another Jewish holocaust? Absolutely not. Lindsey's faulty logic, questionable handling of Scripture, and misrepresentation of the views he attacks suggest that he owes the Christians he has slandered an apology.

It is important to state that I'm not aware of any other serious pre-tribulationist scholar who shares Lindsey's position. Bible scholars and trained theologians recognize that the differences that divide us into pre-tribulationists, post-tribulational premillennialists, amillennialists, and postmillennialists characterize people of goodwill who simply interpret Scripture differently. Serious students of Scripture and theology who happen to be pre-tribulationists tend to be embarrassed by books that presume to date the time of the rapture or characterize anyone who disagrees with them as anti-Semitic.

Are Theonomists Enemies of Democracy?

The charge that theonomists are somehow enemies of democracy appeared in the respected evangelical magazine *Christianity Today*. The source of this charge, author Rodney Clapp, noticed that theonomists were supporters of a theocratic form of government and simply assumed that they were interested in forcing their view on nations like the United States. Clapp should have done a bit more homework.

As Clapp explains theonomy, "In the Reconstructed society, there will be no federal government. Nor will there be a democracy, which Reconstructionists regard as heresy."[17]

One response to Clapp's charges has been given by theonomist Gary DeMar. "Theonomy," DeMar writes, "begins with God's Word as the standard for making policy decisions. At the same time, the theonomist realizes that he lives in a world that is far from the biblical ideal. The theonomist attempts to set forth a developed theoretical biblical model of society. But the theonomist also realizes that the entire model cannot be implemented immediately." DeMar points out the importance of decentralization for theonomists. In other words, the theonomist "model cannot be imposed from the top-down." Theonomists also believe in gradualism, which means that "the model must be embraced by the masses and implemented over time through the democratic process."[18]

In these words, DeMar effectively negates the charge of anti-democracy by specifically denying that the theonomist model can be forcibly imposed on a society from the top down. Some theonomists, then, seem to be committed to a long, slow process that will continue long beyond the life span of any living theonomist.

Theonomist Greg Bahnsen begins his own attempt to set the record straight on the issue of democracy by pointing out that the word *democracy* is a notoriously ambiguous term. He says the word is "susceptible to an incredibly wide range of definitions and connotations." These different senses include,

Bahnsen explains, meanings ranging "from an institution of direct rule by every citizen without mediating representatives to a governmental procedure where representatives are voted in and out of office by the people, to the simple concepts of majority vote or social equality."[19] Any reasonable person, Bahnsen points out, would shun some of these meanings while defending others. In cases where *democracy* is synonymous with mob rule, many Christians might oppose the concept. But where *democracy* means the kind of representative government described in the U.S. Constitution, at least some theonomists, like Bahnsen and DeMar, support it.

Clearly, then, theonomists oppose efforts to force their model of society on any nation. Their preferred model will come into existence only after the vast majority of people in a society have become believers and have *voluntarily* submitted to God's law. There is no way of telling how many generations or how many centuries must pass before this condition will be satisfied. It seems clear that it will not occur in the lifetime of anyone presently alive. Society cannot change, Gary DeMar writes, "unless people change, and the only way people can change is through the regenerating work of the Holy Spirit."[20] Therefore, taking over the government is not a theonomist objective.

Are theonomists enemies of democracy? You decide.

WHY I AM NOT A THEONOMIST

I have spent so much time defending theonomists from false charges that I realize some readers may identify me with theonomy. To forestall that possibility, I'll spend the rest of this chapter discussing why I am not a theonomist. I believe the reader will find that this last section of the chapter raises some interesting questions about the place of Old Testament law in the thinking of New Testament believers.

The crux of the debate over theonomy concerns the

theonomist conviction that biblical law must be applied to all of life. God's law is the standard for both individual and social life. This teaching becomes controversial primarily because theonomists include, within the bounds of what they call "biblical law," elements of the Mosaic civil code that most Christians assume are no longer applicable. I refer here to prescriptions in the Pentateuch that people be executed for things like witchcraft, homosexual activity, and other forms of sexual immorality. If many of these laws were to become legislation, a lot of Americans would find themselves in serious trouble. While Christians oppose the kinds of conduct just mentioned, they have a strong initial resistance to suggestions that such behavior today merits capital punishment.

Fair critics of theonomy must recognize the diversity of the movement. Serious differences now exist among various groups within the larger theonomist camp. As Bahnsen and Gentry state, theonomy "does not represent a movement, but a set of fundamental theological convictions of a distinctive yet general nature, and held by an unorganized group of individual Christians—held in differing ways, for different reasons, and with differing ramifications."[21] In spite of what some theonomists would have us believe, theonomy is not a monolithic movement. Consequently Greg Bahnsen rejects Rousas Rushdoony's "idiosyncratic view of the continuing validity of the laws regarding diet and mixed-fibre clothing," as well as Gary North's "endorsement of stoning as the method of capital punishment even today."[22]

The Theonomic Distinction Between God's Standing Law and Positive Law

Almost all theonomists draw a sharp distinction between standing law and positive law. *Positive law* refers to particular instructions for specific individuals. An example would be God's command to Samuel that he anoint David. Another would be God's command that Israel destroy some of the tribes living in Canaan. God's positive laws are *not* applicable beyond the times and circumstances under which they were given.

God's *standing law* is not subject to such restrictions. Theonomists like Bahnsen understand this second kind of law to be "*policy* directives applicable over time to classes of individuals (e.g., do not kill; children, obey your parents; merchants, have equal measures; magistrates, execute rapists)" and so on.[23] Theonomists insist that standing laws continue to be binding, unless they are rescinded or modified in the New Testament. It is this last point that sets up the major clash between theonomists and pre-tribulationists.

Some pre-tribulationists maintain that all Old Testament laws except those explicitly *certified* in the New Testament have been abrogated.[24] Theonomists counter by maintaining that all standing laws not specifically *rescinded* in the New Testament remain in force.[25] In other words, pre-tribulationists teach that if an Old Testament law isn't *repeated* in the New Testament, then it no longer applies. But theonomists teach that if an Old Testament law isn't *repealed* in the New Testament, then it remains in effect.[26]

Every Jot and Tittle?

In his 1977 book *Theonomy in Christian Ethics*, Greg Bahnsen wrote that "central to the theory and practice of Christian ethics, whether personal or social, is every jot and tittle of God's law as laid down in the revelation of the Older and New Testaments. The Christian is obligated to keep the whole law of God as a pattern of sanctification, and in the realm of human society the civil magistrate is responsible to enforce God's law against public crime."[27] Ever since they were written, these two sentences have functioned as a rallying cry for theonomists. Once this status of Old Testament standing law is settled for Bahnsen, he goes on: "The civil precepts of the Old Testament (standing 'judicial' laws) are a model of perfect social justice for all cultures, even in the punishment of criminals." But then Bahnsen adds a critically important qualification, namely, that "there is plenty of need for interpretation and application."[28]

Bahnsen published this last statement in 1989. In earlier years, theonomists tended to downplay the need for "interpretation and application." It is my impression that during the early days of the theonomist movement—though I must confess that I was not paying much attention then—there was an attempt to present a public face that minimized differences of opinion over these interpretations and applications. Perhaps theonomist writers were so intent on making their case for the continuing relevance of Old Testament standing law that they did little of the hard work of dealing with interpretation and application. Or perhaps the interpretation and application that was done was handled by the same small team of writers, such as Rushdoony, North, and Bahnsen. And no doubt it was easier in those more simple times for theonomists like Bahnsen to boast about how they were the guardians of "every jot and tittle" of God's law.

Whatever the situation may have been in the past, things have changed considerably within the theonomist camp. And Greg Bahnsen has become a major force behind these changes. Bahnsen has realized not only that the task of interpreting and applying Old Testament law can be very difficult, but also that it is creating divisions within the theonomist movement. It is even leading Bahnsen himself to suggest interpretations and applications that appear to conflict with his own 1977 defense of "every jot and tittle" of Old Testament law. Consider the following statement that Bahnsen wrote in 1989:

> It is one thing to realize that we must translate biblical commands about a lost ax (Exodus 23:4) or withholding pay from someone who mows the fields (James 5:4) into terms relevant to our present culture (e.g., about misplaced credit cards or remuneration of factory workers). It is quite another thing altogether to say that such commands carry no ethical authority today! God

obviously communicated to His people in terms of their own day and cultural setting, but what He said to them He fully expects us to obey in our own cultural setting, lest the complete authority of His Word be shortchanged in our lives.[29]

As we wrestle with the problems of interpreting and applying biblical law to the far different situations of our own day, it is important, Bahnsen thinks, that we learn to look for the broader principles that underlie general precepts and specific illustrations. What all this points to, Bahnsen suggests, is our need for common sense when interpreting the Bible. For example, he writes, "The requirement of a rooftop railing (Deuteronomy 22:8), relevant to entertaining on flat roofs in Palestine, teaches the underlying principle of safety precautions (e.g., fences around modern backyard swimming pools), not the obligation of placing a literal battlement upon today's sloped roofs."[30]

The significant move from an application of Deuteronomy 22:8, requiring all Christians to erect rooftop railings on their homes, to one in which we place fences around our swimming pools is a welcome concession to common sense. But it is hard to shake the nagging suspicion that Bahnsen ends up many times with advice that is pretty trivial under the conditions that exist today. Do educated Southern Californians with enough money to afford a swimming pool need Deuteronomy 22:8 to tell them that they ought to have fences around their expensive and dangerous pools? And more to the point, must they learn this from the Bible in such an apparently contrived manner? It looks as though the theonomist would be doing his system a favor by admitting that perhaps Deuteronomy 22:8 is one Old Testament law, though not rescinded in the New Testament, that just isn't needed any more.

One reason theonomists don't make these admissions is because it would undermine their position by introducing a note of relativity to their idea of standing law. If sincere Christians, including sincere theonomists, can disagree over whether some Old Testament law really is an example of standing law, it is difficult to see how theonomy offers more than previous generations of non-theonomic Reformed thinkers who took the Old Testament more seriously than did others. What is wrong with simply admitting that God can prescribe laws for some specific cultural situation where no subsequent applications are intended?

It is unlikely that any sensible theonomist is encouraging a simple-minded imitation of ancient Israel by superimposing *its* laws upon *our* culture. But as John Frame suggests, "Theonomy is not quite as radical as one might have initially supposed. Like the more traditional Reformed theologians [who were not theonomists], the [theonomists] find much in the Old Testament law that we cannot follow literally today."[31]

What set theonomy apart during its earlier history was a sense of radicalness, that is, the feeling that these people were going further than had other Reformed thinkers in their appeal to Old Testament moral and civil principles. We have noticed that this earlier radicalness is being abandoned by more sensible theonomists as they are forced to move closer to a more traditional Reformed position.

There seems to be reason to think that Rousas Rushdoony, the father of the movement, is not too pleased about these recent developments. At the same time that Bahnsen, DeMar, and others are successfully rebutting published attacks on theonomy, Rushdoony may well think that they are giving away the store. Certainly hard-core theonomists (Rushdoony insists on following Old Testament dietary laws and Gary North argues for Old Testament methods of capital punishment) still exude that air of radicalness. It is no longer necessary to go outside the theonomist camp to find people willing to dismiss such talk.

As we've seen, Bahnsen rejects the abiding validity of the Old Testament dietary laws. He does not think it necessary that punishments for crimes accord literally with those identified in the Old Testament. Bahnsen admits that some spiritualizing may be necessary. Given modern technology, there may be no reason to resort to stoning as the preferred method of capital punishment.[32] Bahnsen admits that finding the proper application of some Old Testament practices can be very difficult. Gary DeMar (in personal conversation) admits that he doesn't know how some Old Testament laws might apply today. It seems clear to me that theonomists like Bahnsen and DeMar are moving very close to a more traditional Reformed stance on the Old Testament. In fact, it seems clear that they are moving away from what has been the defining feature of theonomy up to now.

What we may be seeing is the growing recognition on the part of maturing theonomists that the old theonomy is less important than reconstructionism and postmillennialism. As I explained earlier in this chapter, it is possible to be a reconstructionist and a postmillennialist without also being a theonomist. It may only now be dawning on some theonomists that they can have everything *they* want by pursuing a postmillennial reconstructionism and forgetting the hermeneutical oddities that have been a defining feature of earlier theonomy.

Theonomists can be commended for many things: their high view of Scripture; their love of God's Word and God's law; their attention to all of Scripture, including large portions of the Old Testament that many Christians ignore or quickly pass over; their search for a principled approach to understanding and applying the Old Testament; and their desire to fulfill the mandate to love all of God's law. In all of these ways and more, they put many Christians including myself to shame.

But the Achilles heel of their system is found in the relativity and subjectivity that recent work has uncovered in their method of biblical interpretation. This is not to deny that the same problem troubles the rest of us. But theonomists always pretended that this was not a problem *for them*. Now it appears otherwise.

All of the commendable features noted above are still available to theonomists if they turn away from the peculiar excesses of the older theonomist position and align themselves with more traditional Reformed thinkers who were wrestling with the problems of interpreting and applying the Old Testament long before anyone had heard of theonomy. There is no need for ex-theonomists to forfeit their right to fight for dominion in society, since as we've seen, one can be a reconstructionist without also being a theonomist.

CONCLUSION

What have we learned in this chapter? Quite I bit, I hope. For one thing, the people called theonomists don't appear to be dangerous. Efforts to show that they are dangerous do more, I suspect, to dishonor the people raising the charges. But just because theonomists are not dangerous doesn't mean that they're not wrong—at least on some important matters.

We can thank theonomists for forcing the rest of us to face up to the question of what we're going to do with all those laws in the Old Testament. But there is one thing that we non-theonomists cannot do and that is conclude that all those laws must be applied literally to our cultural and social situations. Moreover, as we've seen, this is a conclusion that some theonomist leaders are reaching for themselves.

I suspect that large numbers of theonomists will effectively abandon some of the distinctive features that used to characterize all theonomists and that continue to be the marks of the more extreme. Given the associations the theonomist label has acquired, it would make sense for them to abandon that term as well.

Chapter Nine

THE CONTROVERSY OVER LORDSHIP SALVATION

The debate over what has become known as "lordship salvation" involves the relationship between salvation and obedience. In 1988 the controversy was given new impetus with the appearance of the book *The Gospel According to Jesus* by John F. MacArthur, Jr.[1] MacArthur states that his reason for writing the book was concern over what he saw as evangelical teaching of a defective view of salvation. According to MacArthur, the central claim of his book "is that the gospel summons sinners to yield to Christ's authority."[2]

One major source of the position MacArthur was criticizing was Zane Hodges, author of *The Gospel Under Siege*.[3] Soon after the appearance of MacArthur's book, Hodges published his reply in a book titled *Absolutely Free*.[4] Not to be outdone, another opponent of "lordship salvation," Charles Ryrie, came out with his own response, *So Great Salvation*.[5] All three books sold tens of thousands of copies, which suggests a lot of interest and possibly also a lot of confusion about the subject.

However difficult it may be to sort out the issues in this controversy, the dispute holds important implications for the church's understanding and teaching of the doctrine of salvation.

Other issues involved in this debate include the relationship between faith and works, repentance, legalism, and cheap grace. No feature of this disagreement is trivial or unimportant for Christians who wish to be informed about their faith.

WHAT IS LORDSHIP SALVATION?

Livingston Blauvelt, Jr., defines "lordship salvation" as "the view that for salvation a person must trust Jesus Christ as his Savior from sin and must also commit himself to Christ as Lord of his life, submitting to His sovereign authority."[6] Arthur W. Pink summarized the position: "No one can receive Christ as His Savior while he rejects Him as Lord. Therefore, those who have not bowed to Christ's scepter and enthroned Him in their hearts and lives, and yet imagine that they are trusting Him as Savior, are deceived."[7]

John R. W. Stott, a widely published evangelical author and former rector of All Souls' Church in London, England, made his own commitment to lordship salvation clear when he wrote: "The astonishing idea is current in some circles today that we can enjoy the benefits of Christ's salvation without accepting the challenge of His sovereign Lordship."[8]

As proponents of lordship salvation see things, it is a serious error to separate the acts of receiving Christ as Savior and acknowledging Him as Lord. Opponents of the lordship doctrine, on the other hand, see these as distinct acts. In the second view, one first becomes a Christian via the act of receiving Christ as Savior. Then, following conversion, the Christian may or may not submit to Christ as Lord and Master.

The basic issue in the dispute is whether it is necessary to accept Christ as Lord in order to have Him as one's Savior. The question then becomes, If someone accepts Christ as Savior without also explicitly accepting Him as Lord, is such a person truly saved?

Proponents of the lordship doctrine answer this question

in the negative. Critics of the lordship teaching, on the other hand, accuse it of mixing faith with works in the act of salvation. Proponents of lordship salvation deny this claim. They reject any suggestion that their position entails salvation by works. Justification is by faith alone, they insist. MacArthur writes,

> Let me say as clearly as possible right now that salvation is by God's sovereign grace and grace alone. Nothing a lost, degenerate, spiritually dead sinner can do will in any way contribute to salvation. Saving faith, repentance, commitment, and obedience are all divine works, wrought by the Holy Spirit in the heart of everyone who is saved.

MacArthur continues by claiming,

> Real salvation cannot and will not fail to produce works of righteousness in the life of a true believer. There are no human works in the saving act, but God's work of salvation includes a change of intent, will, desire, and attitude that inevitably produces the fruit of the Spirit. The very essence of God's saving work is the transformation of the will that results in a love for God. Salvation thus establishes the *root* that will surely produce the *fruit*.[9]

WHO ARE ITS OPPONENTS?

Assigning a label to opponents of the lordship doctrine is a difficult task. None of the names suggested by lordship proponents really fit. There is, of course, the old word *antinomian*. But critics of the lordship doctrine object to this term, which literally means "opposed to the law" (of God). Since the term has historically been applied to people who suggested that Christians are totally free from any relationship to God's law and thus free to live any way they choose, the word does have strongly negative connotations. But I think we must give the lordship critics every benefit of the doubt and assume that they wish to avoid the antinomian heresy.

For the sake of discussion, the best labels to use are "supporters" and "proponents" to describe those who defend the lordship doctrine and "critics" and "opponents" to refer to those who do not.

Opponents like Charles Ryrie claim that evangelicals who teach lordship salvation are preachers of a different gospel. Ryrie does not mince words when he says, "The message of faith only and the message of faith plus commitment of life cannot both be the gospel; therefore, one of them is false and comes under the curse of perverting the gospel or preaching another gospel (Gal. 1:6-9)."[10] This is a serious charge.

But supporters of lordship salvation are not the least bit timid in expressing their opinions of the doctrine's opponents. When these critics, MacArthur writes, separate faith from faithfulness,[11] "it leaves the impression that intellectual assent is as valid as wholehearted obedience to the truth. Thus the good news of Christ has given way to the bad news of an insidious easy-believism that makes no moral demands on the lives of sinners. It is not the same message Jesus proclaimed."[12] And so we see that both sides accuse the other of preaching a different gospel, a false gospel!

Why, MacArthur asks, "should we assume that people who live in an unbroken pattern of adultery, fornication, homosexuality, deceit, and every conceivable kind of flagrant excess are truly born again?" And yet, he continues, "that is exactly the assumption Christians of this age have been taught to make. They've been told that the only criterion for salvation is knowing and believing some basic facts about Christ. They hear from the beginning that obedience is optional."[13] MacArthur accuses his opponents of teaching justification without sanctification.

"Faith that does not result in righteous living is dead and cannot save (James 2:14-17)."[14]

Is the position of lordship salvation opponents really as extreme as writers like MacArthur suggest? Let's examine their views. Zane Hodges, in interpreting Jesus' encounter with the woman at the well in John 4, states, "There is no call here for surrender, submission, acknowledgement of Christ's Lordship, or anything else of this kind. A gift is being offered to one totally unworthy of God's favor. And to get it, the woman is required to make no spiritual commitment whatsoever. She is merely invited to ask."[15] Hodges does appear to present salvation as a matter of intellectual assent to the claims of the gospel. But would he agree? We'll see in a moment.

The importance of the dispute should be obvious. Christians have an obligation to present Christ and the gospel in a way that is faithful to the Scriptures. If the lordship doctrine is correct, then many involved in evangelism are doing an incomplete job; they are presenting only half a message. Proponents of lordship salvation are concerned "that an improper, shallow presentation of the Gospel will drive men to a mere psychological or emotional conversion."[16]

As I look back over my own early ministry, I recognize how this controversy affected me, even though at the time, I had no clear idea what was occurring. During my first pastorate, in the Finger Lakes region of New York state, a visiting evangelist held services in the church. As he and I visited in various homes in the community, his approach to evangelism led us into a discussion of the issue. What I did not realize then, and in fact only comprehended after beginning work on this chapter, is that the evangelist's approach to soul-winning paralleled that of authors like Zane Hodges who reject lordship salvation. The evangelist's approach to the unconverted was to invite them to assent intellectually to certain true statements. What lordship proponents would object to was that there was no mention of repentance or commitment. Given this personal history, I must confess that when I read Hodges or Ryrie stating that a person can "have Christ as Savior without having him as Lord,"[17] my first inclination is to dismiss this view as unbiblical. But perhaps a more detailed examination of the critics' arguments will help to put the debate in a different light.

THE MAJOR OBJECTIONS TO LORDSHIP SALVATION

In this section of the chapter, we'll examine the major objections to the lordship doctrine found in the writings of critics. The first is the claim that *lordship salvation mixes faith and works*. If true, this would be a serious charge.

Hodges accuses MacArthur of mixing faith and works in his book *Absolutely Free*.[18] Hodges's main support for his claim is a quotation in which MacArthur states that "obedience is the inevitable manifestation of saving faith." As Hodges reads MacArthur, this is supposed to mean that "without obedience there is no justification and no heaven."[19] Given MacArthur's repeated assurances that he rejects any place for human works in justification, perhaps Hodges misunderstands MacArthur's position. MacArthur does not say in his quote that obedience is the necessary condition for salvation, only that obedience is the inevitable manifestation of salvation. While the first claim would be heretical, the second is quite biblical.

The book of James teaches that faith without works is dead. If a supposedly converted sinner evidences no change following his "conversion," then James teaches there may be some question about the genuineness of that person's faith. So, the proponent of lordship salvation claims he is not adding anything to biblical faith or mixing faith with works. He is only stating what Scripture itself declares, namely, that every genuine conversion ought to be followed by some fruits of regeneration.

One of Hodges's standard arguments is apparent in the

following quote: "Neither Romans 2:6 nor 2:13 even remotely imply that faith inevitably produces works."[20] The proponent of lordship salvation would answer that there is a flaw in this kind of appeal: No author and no text can say everything. Different passages of Scripture emphasize different aspects of the total truth. The fact that other passages of God's inerrant Word do seem to teach that faith inevitably produces works is enough for the lordship side.

As we've seen, Hodges attacks MacArthur for allegedly making human effort an essential part of salvation. But in other places, he turns his guns against MacArthur for doing precisely the opposite, that is, for making salvation entirely the work of a sovereign God.[21]

Now, it is hard for a lordship proponent to see how Hodges can have it both ways. If our salvation is entirely the work of a sovereign God, then nothing we do can help effect that salvation. The two claims do seem logically incompatible. MacArthur makes it perfectly clear that he, unlike Hodges, sides totally with the Reformed position. In MacArthur's words, "Thus salvation cannot be defective in any dimension. As part of His saving work, God will produce repentance, faith, sanctification, yieldedness, obedience, and ultimately glorification. Since He is not dependent on human effort in producing those elements, an experience that lacks any of them cannot be the saving work of God."[22]

In a 1990 article published in the *Journal of the Evangelical Theological Society*, MacArthur locates the source of much of Hodges' position on the relationship between faith and works in his inattention to the following distinction:[23]

1. Faith is *passive* in the sense that God does everything in salvation; the sinner contributes nothing to his own salvation.
2. Faith is *inactive* in the sense that it does not necessarily result in any altered conduct or behavior.

Hodges notes that lordship thinkers like MacArthur hold to view one, so he cannot understand why they emphasize obedience. The reason is that lordship supporters reject view two, which of course also happens to be a description of Hodges' position.

Lordship thinkers claim that Hodges' position understands saving faith as nothing more than mental or intellectual assent to the truth of certain propositions, such as "Christ died for my sins." Consequently, they believe Hodges' position is incapable of doing justice to the danger that such New Testament writers as James saw in the possibility of counterfeit faith or imitation faith. As MacArthur points out,

> Evidently there were some in the early Church who flirted with the notion that faith could be a static, inert, inanimate assent to facts. The book of James, probably the earliest NT epistle, confronts this error. James sounds almost as if he were writing to twentieth-century "no-lordship" advocates. He says that people can be deluded into thinking they believe when in fact they do not, and he says that the single factor that distinguishes counterfeit faith from the real thing is the righteous behavior inevitably produced in those who have authentic faith.[24]

Hodges' view of his position says otherwise:

> The one thing we cannot do, however, is to believe something we don't know about. That is why the apostle Paul declared quite plainly, "And how shall they believe in Him of whom they have not heard?" (Romans 10:14). And he added appropriately, "So then faith comes by hearing, and hearing by the word of God" (10:17).
>
> Does that involve the intellect? Of course! But is

it *mere* intellectual assent? Of course *not*! To describe faith that way is to demean it as a trivial, academic exercise, when in fact it is no such thing.

What faith really is, in biblical language, is receiving the testimony of God. It is the *inward conviction* that what God says to us in the gospel is true. That—and that alone—is saving faith.

MacArthur builds a strong case, however, in a later article, that James himself wrote to counter views like Hodges':

> Is it enough to know and understand and assent to the facts of the gospel—even holding the "inward conviction" that these truths apply to me personally—and yet never shun sin or submit to the Lord Jesus? Is a person who holds that kind of belief guaranteed eternal life? Does such a hope constitute faith in the sense in which Scripture uses the term? James expressly teaches that it does not. Real faith, he says, will produce righteous behavior. And the true character of saving faith may be examined in light of the believer's works.[25]

While good works play no role in any person's becoming a Christian (Romans 3:20,24; 4:5; Ephesians 2:9; Titus 3:5), the Bible makes it plain that they do function as a sign of regeneration (Ephesians 2:10, 5:9; 1 John 2:5). There is a difference in the Bible between a dead faith and a *living* faith. "Does this mean," MacArthur writes, "that all true believers are doers of the Word? Yes. Do they always put the Word in practice? No—or else a pastor's task would be relatively simple. Believers fail, sometimes miserably, as we see in Scripture. But even when they fail, true believers will not altogether cease having the disposition and motivation of one who is a doer."[26]

The major point in James 2 is not that a person is saved by

faith plus works, but that we are saved only through a genuine or living faith as opposed to a counterfeit or dead faith. According to the argument of Hodges and other critics of lordship salvation, the doctrine in effect mixes faith and works, which is a serious misunderstanding of the lordship teaching. At this point the two sides seem at an impasse.

IS LORDSHIP DOCTRINE DETRIMENTAL TO PERSONAL HOLINESS?

Hodges' second argument states that *lordship salvation is detrimental to personal holiness.* "Instead of promoting holiness," Hodges writes, "the doctrine of lordship salvation destroys the very foundation on which true holiness must be built. By returning to the principles of the law, it has forfeited the spiritual power of grace."[27] The lordship proponent would counter again that the grace described in Scripture is quite different.

What Hodges is doing, of course, is accusing MacArthur of the Galatian heresy. Like the error condemned in Galatians, Hodges claims the lordship position "promotes a judgmental and pharisaical spirit within the church," by allegedly teaching that professing believers who have moral or spiritual difficulties are not good enough for heaven. "The fact that a person falls below the moral standards laid down in God's Word is always tragic and deplorable. But it is not necessarily a proof that one is also unsaved."[28] Of course. But because this point is so obvious, no lordship advocate disagrees.

The lordship doctrine, Hodges argues, also "exposes Christians to spiritual defeat. By stripping us of the unconditional certainty that we possess eternal life, it dangerously erodes the solid ground we need beneath our feet."[29] We should pause here and reflect upon Hodges' complete position. Remember that Hodges is the friend of, the advocate for, backslidden Christians. While no lordship advocate denies that genuine Christians may backslide, Hodges defends the professing Christian who shows no fruit—or has fallen into worldliness—from any suggestion that their profession might be less than genuine. Given Hodges' argument, lordship advocates find it incredible that he accuses them of inducing "spiritual *defeat.*" The lordship side would argue that, while Christian leaders should be careful about introducing doubt into any Christian's life, there is also a serious danger of inducing a false confidence, especially in the case of professing believers who show absolutely no signs of regeneration.

At this point the debate is again at an impasse. Hodges argues that his position does not entail "mere intellectual assent" while MacArthur and other lordship proponents defend their side against the charge that they promote either a pharisaical spirit or spiritual defeat in the sanctification of the believer.

Again, both sides are confident of their positions and both believe they are right. No unity or common ground seems possible.

Let's now turn to some key ingredients in the debate that shed further important light on each side.

SEVERAL CRUCIAL ISSUES

In an effort to move even closer to the biblical truth on this matter, let us examine two crucial issues: repentance and the meaning of the term *Lord.*

Repentance

According to Hodges, repentance is *not* a condition for salvation. In his view of things, "the call to repentance is *broader than* the call to eternal salvation. It is rather a call to *harmony* between the creature and his creator, a call to *fellowship* between sinful men and women and a forgiving God."[30]

On the other side, lordship proponents can count on quite a few cases in which the biblical teaching about repentance is spread among a number of passages. Different texts emphasize different points.

Hodges' view seems to turn on two critical points: (1) that there's a clear distinction between faith and repentance such that repentance cannot be made a condition for eternal life, and (2) the meaning of the Greek word *metanoeo*, the word translated "to repent" in the New Testament. Hodges writes:

> It is an extremely serious matter when the biblical distinction between faith and repentance is collapsed and when repentance is thus made a condition for eternal life. For under this perception of things the New Testament doctrine of faith is radically rewritten and held hostage to the demand for repentance. No wonder one scholar in the writings of Calvin has been moved to assert:
>
> Those who teach that repentance precedes faith, and make faith and forgiveness conditional upon repentance, fail to see that theirs is a position parallel to the Roman doctrine of penance that Calvin so strongly opposed [M. Charles Bell, *Calvin and Scottish Theology* (Edinburgh, Scotland: Handsel, 1985), page 39, n. 208)].
>
> There can be no compromise on this point if we wish to preserve and to proclaim the biblical truth of *sola fide*. To make repentance a condition for eternal salvation is nothing less than a regression toward Roman Catholic dogma.
>
> "But," someone will say, "does not the Bible also declare God's demand for repentance?" Indeed it does, and perhaps nowhere more forcefully than in Acts 17:30 where Paul declares: "And these times of ignorance God overlooked, but now commands *all men everywhere to repent*" (italics added).
>
> Can this declaration be harmonized with *sola*

fide—"faith alone"? Yes, it can, since the Bible is never internally contradictory. And the harmonization is really very easy and natural. How?

Simply put, we may say this: the call to faith represents the call to eternal salvation. The call to repentance is the call to enter into harmonious relations with God.[31]

Hodges believes that while genuine repentance *may* precede salvation, it *need not* do so. But where I find his argument lacking is in his view of the meaning of the word *repentance*. He writes:

Originally, these Greek words meant to change one's mind. But the standard Greek-English dictionary does not list any New Testament passage where the meaning "to change one's mind" actually occurs.[32]

But this is not what the Bauer-Arndt-Gingrich Greek Lexicon states (BAG—the "standard" one Hodges refers to in his endnotes). The BAG entry on *metanoia* (Greek noun, "repentance") and *metanoeo* (Greek verb, "to repent") lists a number of specific entries where these words do, in the Greek New Testament, refer specifically to the act of changing one's mind. Page 513 (fourth revised and augmented edition) gives "change one's mind" as the primary meaning of the word *metanoeo*, then adds a number of additions to that meaning, but never changes the primary meaning of the word. There are also a number of entries under the noun *metanoia*, which refer to "conversion," "a turning away from dead works," "repentance that leads to God," and "turning about." All of these meanings seem to derive from the basic meaning of "a change of mind." And a whole passel of New Testament passages are cited entailing these meanings including: Hebrews 6:1, Matthew 3:8, Luke 3:8 and 15:7 (where BAG denotes the meaning as "repentance for conversion").[33]

Even giving Hodges the benefit of the doubt on his view, at the very least, one can see why MacArthur, J. I. Packer, and many others would take issue with him on the meaning of repentance. On the lordship proponent's view, Hodges has misread the basic meaning of the term and placed an unnecessary limitation on the word's meanings.

Interestingly, Hodges' contention that repentance is not necessarily bound up in salvation was not shared by his mentor, Lewis Sperry Chafer, who wrote:

> Too often, when it is asserted—as it is here—that repentance is not to be added to belief as a separate requirement for salvation, it is assumed that by so much the claim has been set up that repentance is *not* necessary to salvation. Therefore, it is as dogmatically stated as language can declare, that repentance is essential to salvation and that none could be saved apart from repentance, but it is included in believing and could not be separated from it.[34]

Both sides agree that godly repentance should not be confused with emotionalism. As Kenneth Gentry explains, "The necessary element in salvatory repentance is a true recognition of one's evil state and a decided resolve to forsake sin and thrust oneself at Christ's mercy. Certainly great sorrow may be involved, but it will be sorrow because of the recognition of Christ's holiness displayed against the background of one's own sinfulness."[35]

James Packer concurs: "The repentance that Christ requires of His people consists in a settled refusal to set any limits to the claims which He may make on their lives. . . . Where there is no clear knowledge, and hence no realistic recognition of the real claims that Christ makes, there can be no repentance, and therefore no salvation."[36]

John MacArthur clearly aligns himself with those who

understand Scripture to teach a role for repentance in salvation. He argues that repentance "involves a recognition of one's utter sinfulness and a turning from self and sin to God (c.f. 1 Thessalonians 1:9). Far from being a human work, it is the inevitable result of *God's* work in a human heart. And it always represents the end of any human attempt to earn God's favor. It is much more than a mere change of mind—it involves a complete change of heart, attitude, interest, and direction. It is a conversion in every sense of the word."[37]

MacArthur is surely right when he argues that "repentance is not merely being ashamed or sorry over sin, although genuine repentance always involves an element of remorse. It is a redirection of the human will, a purposeful decision to forsake all unrighteousness and pursue righteousness instead. Nor is repentance merely a human work. It is, like every element of redemption, a sovereignly bestowed gift of God. . . . Above all, repentance is *not* a pre-salvation attempt to set one's life in order. The call to repentance is not a command to make sin right *before* turning to Christ in faith. Rather it is a command to recognize one's lawlessness and hate it, to turn one's back on it and flee to Christ, embracing Him with wholehearted devotion."[38]

The Meaning of "Lord"

Opponents of lordship salvation do not deny that Christ is Lord or that acknowledging His lordship is necessary to salvation. Romans 10:9-10 is simply too clear for any Christian to ignore. They do, however, draw a distinction between what they call the objective and subjective lordship of Jesus.

Objective lordship refers to Jesus' deity. In this sense, Jesus is already Lord. In the objective sense, the lordship of Christ cannot be denied without rejecting the essential Christian teaching that Jesus has always been God the Son.

The subjective lordship of Jesus refers to the need for people to surrender to Him as Master. Charles Ryrie utilizes the distinction in trying to avoid the lordship doctrine by claiming that Romans 10:9-10 has nothing to do with Christ's subjective lordship. It concerns only His deity. "To believe that Jesus (the man) is Lord (God) and that He is alive (which means that He died) results in righteousness and salvation."[39] But when it comes to the question of Christ's subjective lordship, Ryrie retreats to tentativeness. Is Christ Lord in the sense of being God? Yes, says Ryrie. But is Christ not also to be Lord in the subjective sense? Here all Ryrie can say is, "Of course He should be, sometimes is, and sometimes is partly so."[40]

While no one can be a believer without acknowledging the objective lordship of Christ (Romans 10:9-10), lordship critics like Ryrie and Hodges insist that one *can* be a believer without acknowledging Christ's lordship in the subjective sense, that is, without actually acknowledging Him to be Lord or Master.[41]

Kenneth Gentry's reply to this line of thinking is instructive. First, the fact that "the linguistic evidence points quite strongly to the conclusion that *kurios* [Greek, 'Lord'] emphasizes controlling authority. When used of Christ in the frequent Gospel preaching of Acts and the Epistles, it most certainly has to do with the acceptance of Jesus Christ as Lord [in Ryrie's 'subjective sense'] to be Savior." Moreover, Gentry continues, "when Christ is preached as Lord and Savior, the term Lord, or some term expressing rulership, always occurs first for emphasis. See: Luke 1:46-47; Acts 5:31; 2 Peter 1:11; 2:20; 3:18."[42]

John 20:28 is especially relevant in this disagreement. When Thomas saw the risen Christ, he cried out, "My Lord and my God!" If one adopts the position of Ryrie and Hodges, Thomas said nothing more than "My God and my God." The lordship position makes much more sense of this verse, interpreting Thomas' famous utterance as "My Master and my God."[43] Gentry reasons, "When Christ is believed upon or into, it is His Person which is accepted for salvation. Thus, Christ, being the Lord comes into the heart of the believer as Lord and

Master. To omit Christ's office as Lord in the Gospel message is weak evangelistic preaching."[44] I agree.

CONCLUSION

S. Lewis Johnson, Jr., published an important article in *Christianity Today* in which he attempted to adjudicate the dispute between MacArthur and Hodges. I will not take the time to summarize all of his article. But at the end, Johnson drew seven conclusions, which we should review in detail.[45]

First, "it is true that one must confess the lordship of Christ to be saved. Only a sovereign God can save sinners, and the calling on the Lord for mercy is an implicit recognition of his Lordship and of his right of control over us." On this first point, Johnson sides with the supporters of lordship salvation. The point he makes should be beyond dispute.

Second, Johnson insists that the sinner's confession of the lordship of Christ cannot be a shallow profession; it must be genuine. Once again, then, Johnson has no problem with the position of lordship salvation.

In his third point, Johnson explains that "the preeminent term by which salvation is received is *faith*, or *belief*." It is obvious that Johnson views repentance and faith as inseparable. When we understand this correctly, he continues, what we are left with "is not easy believism; in fact, such faith can only be given by God (Ephesians 2:8-9; 1 Corinthians 12:3). It was Jesus himself who said to Jairus, 'Only believe, and she shall be well' (Luke 8:50). The Gospel of John was written to induce faith, and its demand is for faith alone (John 20:30-31)."

In a letter to the editor of *Christianity Today* published two issues later, John MacArthur indicated his solid agreement with Johnson's statement of this point. Since Johnson sides with the lordship position on repentance in this same paragraph, it seems best to regard the third point as another nod in the direction of the lordship position.

Johnson's fourth point begins with an allusion to the Westminster Confession, which teaches that "the realization of Christ's Lordship in growing obedience and submission to his will is the work of sanctification, not justification. The two great teachings [of justification and sanctification] must not be confounded, or the peril of mixing things that differ threatens us." On this matter, Johnson's position accords precisely with that of the lordship salvation advocates.

Johnson's fifth point returns to the teaching of the Westminster Confession, to what it states about the relationship between sanctification and saving faith. Johnson writes, "Christians may *for a time* live in carnality, but only for a time, since divine discipline, which may become severe enough to necessitate physical death, is applied by God (1 Corinthians 5:5, 11:29-30). The term *the carnal Christian*, therefore, is not a category of a Christian acceptable to God, nor does it represent a permanent status in the Christian life." Once again, MacArthur (in his previously noted letter) expresses his total agreement with this point.

But this brings us to Johnson's sixth point where, for the first time, he appears to side with the lordship critics. In Johnson's words, "To insist on a complete submission to God's will as necessary for salvation is unsupported by not only the Gospel of John, but also the Book of Acts."

However, in his aforementioned letter, MacArthur disassociates himself from the position described in Johnson's sixth point. MacArthur concurs that a "total commitment of one's life to Christ in all of life's details is impossible." Who of us knows any Christian who has attained *total* commitment? Even though Jesus called for complete surrender, our fleshly nature always results in something far short of what God demands.

All of this brings us to Johnson's seventh and final point where, once again, he and supporters of the lordship doctrine agree. As Johnson explains, "It is sounder and simpler to keep to Paul's invitation as delivered to the Philippian jailer,

'Believe on the Lord Jesus, and you shall be saved, you and your household' (Acts 16:31, NASB). If we keep in mind that the Lord Jesus is he who has offered himself as a propitiatory substitutionary sacrifice for sinners, and if we remember that saving faith comprehends knowledge, assent, and trust, and if we see that the new life and standing given in justification must issue in a new submission to God's will, then we shall have our gospel thinking in order."

Johnson's recognition that regeneration must of necessity manifest itself in "submission to God's will" is the very point to which supporters of lordship salvation have wanted to draw attention.

To close this chapter on a note of unity, even Charles Ryrie once affirmed the very same point when he asked,

> Can a non-working, dead, spurious faith save a person?
> James is not saying that we are saved by works, but
> that a faith that does not produce good works is a dead
> faith. . . . Unproductive faith cannot save, because it
> is not genuine faith. Faith and works are like a two-
> coupon ticket to heaven. The coupon of works is not
> good for passage, and the coupon of faith is not valid if
> detached from works.[46]

If both sides of our dispute would affirm what Ryrie states in the previous paragraph, the controversy would be laid to rest. I am confident that MacArthur, Packer, Stott, and others on the lordship side agree. Unless Ryrie has changed his mind, he agrees. I hope Zane Hodges will agree as well.

Chapter Ten

THE CONTROVERSY OVER THE END TIMES: WHAT DOES THE BIBLE REALLY SAY?

❖

While browsing through my local newspaper not long ago, I came across an advertisement announcing that a well-known television preacher would be in town to present a series of seven messages on Bible prophecy. "Are You Ready for the End Times?" asked the large print across the top of the advertisement. I chose not to attend the conference since I knew what the speaker's message would be. When she spoke, huge crowds listened hopefully to her descriptions of the coming rapture of the church and to details about the Antichrist who would arise during the horrible years of the tribulation period.

I fear that crowds so large would not have come to hear seven messages about the cross of Christ. Christians today are usually much more fascinated by speculative details of Bible prophecy than by any serious study of how God's redemptive work for them in the past made possible their salvation from sin.

The same quandary exists in the area of Christian publishing. Few books about important Christian doctrines sell enough copies to recover the costs of publication. But let some crisis arise in the Middle East and watch Christians purchase books about Bible prophecy in huge quantities. This was true, for example, during the Gulf War. Several books quickly appeared with pictures of Saddam Hussein on the cover and promises that the reader would understand where Iraq and Babylon fit into the parameters of Bible prophecy. Some were printed in excess of one-million copies. Now that the excitement is over, many of these books lay forgotten in hundreds of thousands of homes.

Many believers seem to ignore the fact that hundreds of books in this century have capitalized on Christians' gullibility. The rogues' gallery of possible antichrists has included every international thug from Hitler and Mussolini to Gorbachev and Hussein.

THE MAJOR OPTIONS

As we've mentioned briefly, Christian thinking about the end times has crystallized into three major positions, all centering around differing interpretations of the thousand-year period of time described in Revelation 20. Since the Latin word for thousand is *mille*, this period is usually called "the millennium."

The position called *pre*millennialism holds that the Second Coming of Christ comes *before* the thousand years described in Revelation 20. Premillennialists typically take the number "one thousand" literally and teach that Jesus Christ will rule and reign from a literal throne on planet Earth for a thousand years, following which a brief rebellion against His authority will be ended (20:7-10). Then will follow the great white throne judgment (20:11-15) and the new heaven and new earth described in Revelation 21.

The position known as *post*millennialism was already covered in considerable detail in my earlier chapter on the theonomist movement. Stated simply, a postmillennialist believes that the famous text in Revelation 19:11-16 refers not to the Second Coming of Christ at the end of the world, but is instead a symbolic picture of Christ and His gospel triumphing over the world. Postmillennialists believe in a future victory of the church over evil based on God's marvelous blessing of the preaching of His truth. In this view of things, Jesus Christ will return *after* this victory by His church.

The third view known as *a*millennialism interprets the thousand years of Revelation in a figurative way. For an amillennialist, there will be no literal thousand-year reign of Christ on earth. When this age ends, the Second Coming of Christ will be followed immediately by the great white throne judgment where God will finally and forever separate believers from unbelievers. The thousand years of Revelation 20, amillennialists insist, must be taken symbolically. The picture of Christ ruling and reigning should be understood as a reference to what I call later in this chapter the "church triumphant" or the church in heaven.

PRE-TRIBULATIONISM

Most TV preachers and nearly all of the books about Bible prophecy these days share a common set of beliefs on what the Bible teaches about the end times. It is a variety of premillennialism called pre-tribulationism.

According to this understanding of Bible prophecy, the next event in the prophetic calendar allegedly is the rapture of the church. While this event resembles the Second Coming of Christ, pre-tribulationists distinguish the rapture from the Second Coming. In the rapture, Christ will return in the air for the entire Christian church. Dead believers will be resurrected and then caught up in the air, where they will join with living believers who have been transformed and lifted bodily out of the world.

None of this will be visible to the unbelieving world, which will be left behind following the rapture. All that unbelievers will know is that suddenly every Christian in the world will have disappeared. The rapture will not only mark the end of what is called the church age, it will also usher in the most terrible period of time the world has ever known: the great tribulation. Thus, this scenario—of the rapture taking place before the tribulation—is called the pre-tribulation rapture.

A powerful, evil world leader known as the Antichrist will then gain control of things. People who become believers during the tribulation will suffer terrible persecution; many thousands of them will be martyred. This information has often frightened people into making hasty decisions for Christ now, in order to avoid the sufferings of the tribulation to come.

The world will experience numerous natural catastrophes (famines, plagues, and earthquakes) along with the war that will finally end all wars. At the end of the seven-year tribulation period, the armies of the world will gather at a place in Palestine called Armaggedon. At this time, Christ will return (this is the *true* Second Coming) with the armies of heaven (believers who were raptured), destroy the wicked, and set up an earthly kingdom for one-thousand years (the millennium). Pre-tribulationists say the biblical support for this scenario is found in chapters 4–20 of the book of Revelation.

One reason for the widespread acceptance of this view of the end times is its prominence in the footnotes of the *Scofield Reference Bible*. It seems safe to say that the vast majority of the approximately fifty million evangelical Christians in the United States accept some version of this teaching. I would not be exaggerating to suggest that 90 percent of these people think the scenario I presented above is *the biblical teaching* about the end times.

What If the Majority Is Wrong?

As every wise Christian knows, you cannot determine the truth of a position by counting noses. The majority can be wrong; indeed, even a huge majority can be wrong.

I'll be direct. There is much about the situation I've been describing that disturbs me. The fact that I used to believe this picture of the end times myself, though I now reject it, is really the least of my concerns. What bothers me the most is the probability that, of the millions of evangelical Christians who accept this picture of the end times, few ever step back and ask whether the Bible actually teaches these things. Almost all of the people talking about these ideas are parroting opinions that they have *never* seriously thought through for themselves or compared with other evangelical views.

As I've said, the odds are that nine out of every ten people who read this book accept what is called the pre-tribulation picture of the end times. If you do, this means that you believe that the next prophetic event to occur will be the sudden rapture of the church, followed by the seven-year tribulation period with all of its accompanying horrors, followed by the Second Coming that will in turn be followed by the millennium. In all likelihood, you, my reader, accept this way of thinking. But why do you accept it? Have you carefully explored all the available options offered by careful students of Scripture and come to this one view? Or is this the *only* position you've been exposed to?

Now, of course, many people can refer to biblical texts that apparently support various contentions of the pre-tribulation view of things. Did not Jesus warn about the great tribulation in Matthew 24? Isn't there the question of seven missing years in Daniel's "seventieth week"? What about all the events described in Revelation 4–20? Personally, I don't find the pre-tribulation interpretation quite that easy.

We Need to Examine Our Thinking Patterns
One important lesson we can learn is the way in which Christians may unwittingly accept a particular pattern of thinking. Once that pattern gains control, it becomes natural for them to group a few passages of Scripture together and interpret them in a certain way. In a sense, something very much like this happens in the case of people who fall into the clutches of cults like the Jehovah's Witnesses. First they accept a certain pattern

of ideas, then they allow that mind-set to determine how they interpret various passages of Scripture.

I am not suggesting, of course, that a pre-tribulation view of Bible prophecy is heresy like the teachings of the Watchtower Society are. I am only stating that there is always a danger that what Christians think the Bible teaches about some issue or other is in fact an idea that is being imposed upon the text.

In the rest of this chapter I'd like to help the reader step back a bit from the widely accepted view and consider other ways of thinking about these things. What can you possibly lose? At the very least, you may discover that the pre-tribulation picture of the end times still makes the most sense. Only now you will have thought through your position for yourself. Instead of being an unchallenged, unreflective adherent of the view, you will have reasons for holding your position, having compared it to another view. If, on the other hand, the reader finds reasons to think the common view may be unbiblical and therefore wrong, has not something important been gained?

In the rest of this chapter I'm going to ask you to reflect on six questions. As you think about these questions, keep your Bible handy. When I give Bible references without quoting the passage, take the time to read the verses carefully. After all, what we're seeking here is information about what the *Bible* really teaches about the end times. Because I've already said so much about postmillennialism in an earlier chapter, the rest of my discussion will contrast pre-tribulationism with an amillennial understanding of the end times. Details of both positions will become clearer as we proceed.

QUESTION ONE: WHAT IS THE DIFFERENCE BETWEEN THE CHURCH MILITANT AND THE CHURCH TRIUMPHANT?

The terms *the church militant* and *the church triumphant* ought to be part of every modern Christian's vocabulary. The church militant refers to the church on earth. The term also refers to the church at war, in the sense that it is involved in spiritual combat "against the rulers, against the authorities, against the powers of this dark world and against the spiritual forces of evil in the heavenly realms" (Ephesians 6:12). The church militant is what's in view whenever we sing "Onward Christian Soldiers."

The church triumphant refers to the victorious church in heaven; it is the church at rest. When the book of Revelation describes believers being persecuted and martyred for their faith (12:11-17), it is talking about the church militant. When Revelation refers to believers who are ruling and reigning with Christ (7:9-17, 20:4), it is describing the church triumphant.

Obviously, these two divisions of the church exist side by side. The writer of Hebrews reminds those of us who are still members of the church militant that the race we run and the battles we fight occur in the presence of a great cloud of witnesses, the church triumphant, who ran the race and fought the battles before us (12:1). When believers die, they leave the church militant and join the church triumphant and victorious (2 Timothy 4:6-8).

Because pre-tribulationists believe that chapters 4–19 of the book of Revelation deal with the tribulation and also believe that the church will not be on earth during this time, they understandably claim that the church cannot be found in Revelation 4–19. I disagree. I believe the church militant is clearly present in these chapters, symbolized by the two witnesses in Revelation 11 and by the woman and her seed in chapter 12. The church triumphant is symbolized by the twenty-four elders in chapter 4 and in the following passage from chapter 7:

> After this I looked and there before me was a great
> multitude that no one could count, from every nation,
> tribe, people and language, standing before the throne
> and in front of the Lamb. They were wearing white

robes and were holding palm branches in their hands. And they cried out in a loud voice: "Salvation belongs to our God, who sits on the throne, and to the Lamb." (verses 9-10)

As the passage continues, someone asks who the people in white robes are and where they came from. They are described in the following terms: "These are they who have come out of the great tribulation; they have washed their robes and made them white in the blood of the Lamb" (verse 14). Do not be confused by the fact that these people have come out of the great tribulation. Amillennialists see this not as a reference to a seven-year long tribulation period but to the two-thousand-year long struggle of the church militant against trials, persecution, and suffering. The identity of these blood-bought, redeemed people is given in the last three verses of the chapter (verses 15-17).

"They are," the passage goes on to say, "before the throne of God and serve him day and night in his temple; and he who sits on the throne will spread his tent over them. Never again will they hunger; never again will they thirst. The sun will not beat upon them, nor any scorching heat. For the Lamb at the center of the throne will be their shepherd; he will lead them to springs of living water. And God will wipe away every tear from their eyes" (7:15-17).

There is no more magnificent passage in all of Scripture that describes the blessed state of the redeemed. I believe that to apply this text to anything other than the church triumphant, the church at rest, does an enormous injustice to the text.

QUESTION TWO: WHAT IS THE DIFFERENCE BETWEEN THE WRATH OF MAN AND THE WRATH OF GOD?

The "wrath of man" is a reference to such human-caused evils as war, persecution, and martyrdom. The "wrath of God" refers to divine judgment and punishment. Joel 3:9-16 discusses both types of wrath.

First, the prophet Joel describes the wrath of man:

> Proclaim this among the nations: Prepare for war! Rouse the warriors! Let all the fighting men draw near and attack. Beat your plowshares into swords and your pruning hooks into spears. Let the weakling say, "I am strong!" Come quickly, all you nations from every side, and assemble there. Bring down your warriors, O Lord! "Let the nations be roused; let them advance into the Valley of Jehoshaphat, for there I will sit to judge all the nations on every side. Swing the sickle, for the harvest is ripe. Come, trample the grapes, for the winepress is full and the vats overflow—so great is their wickedness!" (3:9-13)

Then Joel begins to discuss the wrath of God:

> Multitudes, multitudes in the valley of decision! For the day of the Lord is near in the valley of decision. The sun and moon will be darkened, and the stars no longer shine. The Lord will roar from Zion and thunder from Jerusalem; the earth and the sky will tremble. But the Lord will be a refuge for his people, a stronghold for the people of Israel. (3:14-16)

In the Bible, the wrath of man is always associated with tribulation while the wrath of God is always associated with the Day of the Lord (Joel 3:14-16; Zephaniah 1:14-18, 2:1-3). It is no accident or coincidence that the wrath of man always precedes the wrath of God. The wrath and judgment of God that are to be manifested on the Day of the Lord are, among other things, God's judgment against those wicked men who have dared to touch His anointed.

God never promised His church deliverance from the wrath of man (tribulation). Instead, we find warnings in the Bible, such as these: "In this world you will have trouble" (John 16:33); "we must go through many hardships to enter the kingdom of God" (Acts 14:22). (See also 2 Corinthians 1:4; 1 Thessalonians 3:4; 2 Thessalonians 1:4,6; Revelation 1:9; 2:10; 7:14).

God *has* promised His church deliverance from His wrath. (See John 3:36; Romans 5:9; Ephesians 5:6; 1 Thessalonians 1:10, 5:9; Revelation 6:16-17, 11:18, 16:19, 19:15).

Since God's Word guarantees that His church will suffer tribulation throughout its history on earth, does it not make sense to conclude that the great tribulation out of which the redeemed of Revelation 7 are said to come is a description of the entire period of time between the first and second comings of Christ?

QUESTION THREE: WHAT IF THERE IS NO FUTURE SEVEN-YEAR TRIBULATION PERIOD?

Many Christians who accept the pre-tribulationist scheme of things might be astounded if they realized that amillennialists regard the biblical support for the supposed seven-year tribulation period as flimsy.

Many pre-tribulationists believe they can marshall a clear, careful case from Scripture in support of the teaching that a future seven-year tribulation period will be preceded by the rapture and ended by the Second Coming. The major links in the pre-tribulation argument reduce to three: Jesus' Olivet discourse, especially Matthew 24:21 that warns of "great tribulation" (KJV); the assumption that Revelation 4–19 is a description of the tribulation period; and the account of seventy weeks of years in Daniel 9:24-27. Because of its importance, I will devote my initial attention to the passage in Daniel.

Daniel's Prophecy of the Seventy Weeks

Daniel 9:24-27 introduces a period of 490 years under the symbolism of seventy weeks. Since a week has seven days, seventy weeks times seven yields 490 units of something. No one doubts that Daniel is talking about 490 years. The starting point for the 490 years is "the issuing of a decree to restore and rebuild Jerusalem" (9:24). By the time sixty-nine weeks (or 483 years) have passed, something significant will have happened. Daniel identified that event as the coming of "the Anointed One, the ruler" (9:25). This last phrase must be a reference to the Messiah or the Christ (Hebrew and Greek respectively, "anointed one"). In other words, Daniel is saying, sixty-nine weeks or 483 years must pass from the decree that allowed the exiled Jews to return to Jerusalem to the appearance of the Messiah or the Christ.

Everyone who has studied the writings of pre-tribulationists knows that something very strange occurs in their interpretation of Daniel's seventy weeks: They drive a wedge between the sixty-ninth and the seventieth weeks. Even though there is absolutely no hint in the text of any interruption of the progression of the 490 years, all pre-tribulationists insist that there is a gap between the end of the sixty-ninth week and the start of the seventieth week. Since they believe that the entire church age (by now, almost 2,000 years and counting) fits into this gap, it is obviously a fairly significant interruption.

It is worth considering what would happen if we did not allow for such an interruption in the passage, if we refused to read into Daniel's prophecy this rather outlandish gap of some 2,000 years between the sixty-ninth and the seventieth week. Many scholars' readings of Daniel certainly suggest that the entire period of 490 years was to occur without interruption.

But there is a related problem with the pre-tribulationist handling of Daniel 9:24,27. Pre-tribulationists insist on reading verses 24 and 27 in a way that prevents the verses from describing events that occurred during or shortly after the 490 years. Hence, they could argue, the prophecies of the seventieth week must still be unfilled; therefore, the seventieth week must still belong to the future. And since the seventieth week just happens to be seven years long, we conveniently have a missing period of seven years in God's prophetic time clock. It is just a short hop and a skip from all this to the belief in a future seven-year tribulation period. Or is it?

The quickest way to see why I disagree with the pre-tribulationists' handling of Daniel's seventy weeks is simply to read Daniel 9:24-27 for yourself. Here is what verse 24 says: "Seventy 'sevens' [that is 490 years] are decreed for your people and your holy city to finish transgression, to put an end to sin, to atone for wickedness, to bring in everlasting righteousness, to seal up vision and prophecy and to anoint the most holy One."[1] It takes no great imagination to recognize how everything mentioned in this verse was fulfilled in the atoning work of Christ during His first coming. Jesus put an end to sin, He atoned for human wickedness, He made the righteousness of God available to all sinners, He fulfilled the prophecies regarding the Messiah; and certainly, the anointing of the Holy One is an unmistakable reference to the Messiah or the Christ. Nothing in verse 24 obliges us to continue to look to the future for the eventual fulfillment of anything mentioned in the verse. To miss the Jesus-connection in verse 24 is to miss one of the great Old Testament prophecies dealing with the saving work of Jesus Christ.

Verse 26 then states that sometime after the sixty-ninth week, in other words, during the seventieth week, "the Anointed One [the Messiah again] will be cut off, but not for himself."[2] This is clearly a reference to the death of the Messiah and to the fact that He died for others.

This brings us to verse 27 where the first word is "he." A great deal hangs on finding the correct referent of this word. Pre-tribulationists insist that the subject of verse 27 is the ruler mentioned in verse 26 "who will come [and] destroy the city

[Jerusalem] and the sanctuary." Therefore, they read verse 27 as an account of what the Antichrist (the presumed "ruler" of verse 26) will do during the tribulation period, that is, the future seventieth week. But amillennialists believe any attempts to make the ruler of verse 26 the proper referent of the "he" beginning verse 27 is a mistake, both grammatically and exegetically. For one thing, the word *ruler* is not the subject of the previous verse, which actually refers to "the people of the ruler." Therefore, the word *he* must refer back to "the Anointed One" of verse 26.

So we should read verse 27 as an account of what the *Messiah* will do before the end of the seventy weeks. And here is what verse 27 says: "He [the Messiah] will confirm a covenant with many for one 'week.' In the middle of the 'week' [period of seven years] he will put an end to sacrifice and offering."[3] Amillennialists believe, then, that verse 27 does not refer to the machinations of the Antichrist who will enter into a covenant he doesn't intend to keep, and who will then terminate Jewish sacrifices in a rebuilt temple in Jerusalem. Pre-tribulationists predict those events must happen during the tribulation for no other reason than their interpretation of Daniel 9:27. On the contrary, Daniel is talking about the new covenant or new testament that the Christ will establish with many, a covenant that will forever end the need for the Jewish sacrificial system.[4] The rest of the passage is a clear reference to the horrors during the destruction of Jerusalem that will occur sometime after the end of the seventy weeks.

For amillennialists, the conclusion is clear. We see no suggestion of a gap between the sixty-ninth week and the seventieth week of Daniel. Moreover, everything in Daniel's prophecy was fulfilled during the public ministry of Jesus and the destruction of Jerusalem sometime later. Therefore, we are not still waiting for the seventieth week of Daniel to happen. And there is no future seven-year period of time in which the Antichrist will cause a restored sacrificial system in a rebuilt Jewish temple to cease. Thus, amillennialists contend, the major plank in the elaborate scenario that is the pre-tribulationist understanding of a future seven-year tribulation period collapses.

Allusions to the Tribulation in the New Testament

But, some will ask, what about the references in the book of Revelation to 1260 days and "a time, times and a half a time," apparent allusions to a period of time that is three and a half years long? Surely, some people reason, this specifies half of the seven-year tribulation period.

It remains a source of enormous puzzlement to amillennialists why, in a book noted for its symbolism, anyone would determine that the numbers of Revelation must be taken literally. To me, the most natural interpretation of the 1260 days or three and a half years in Revelation is that it is an obvious allusion to the years of drought that occurred during the ministry of the prophet Elijah. As the book of James reminds us, "Elijah was a man just like us. He prayed earnestly that it would not rain, and it did not rain on the land for three and a half years" (5:17).

But if Daniel 9 and the book of Revelation do not teach a future seven-year period of tribulation, what was Jesus referring to when He said, "For then shall be great tribulation, such as was not since the beginning of the world to this time, no, nor ever shall be" (Matthew 24:21, KJV)?

For one thing, it is helpful at this point to consult other major translations. What the *King James Version* refers to as "great tribulation" is more accurately described in the *New International Version* simply as a time of "great distress." Amillennialists assert that Jesus was referring to a time of great trouble that would arise after the events described in earlier verses; He was *not* referring to a seven-year period that pre-tribulationists call the great tribulation.

Every experienced student of Scripture knows that this passage is extremely difficult to interpret. But the key to understanding the entire message lies in Matthew 24:2-3. Jesus began by referring to the temple in Jerusalem (and other buildings) and said, "I tell you the truth, not one stone here will be left on another; every one will be thrown down" (24:2). The disciples then asked Jesus two questions: "Tell us . . . when will this happen [that is, when will Jerusalem be destroyed?], and what will be the sign of your coming and of the end of the age?" (24:3).

The rest of Matthew 24 is Jesus' answer to these two separate questions. There is nothing through at least Matthew 24:26 that requires us to look beyond the events surrounding the destruction of Jerusalem in AD 70 as the answer to the first question. Consequently, there is no need to assume that the "tribulation" (KJV) or "great distress" (NIV) mentioned in verse 21 is anything other than the horrible calamities that befell the inhabitants of Judea during those terrible days.

However we handle the difficult exegetical problems of the rest of this discourse, amillennialists believe, this much is clear: The famous reference to "great tribulation" in the *King James Version* translation of verse 21 has nothing to do with any seventieth week of Daniel that supposedly still lies in the future. It refers simply to the horrible events that occurred during the siege and eventual destruction of Jerusalem in AD 70.

In this section, we have been considering the question, *What if there is no future seven-year tribulation period?* We have seen that amillennialists believe that the major texts appealed to in support of a future seven-year tribulation teach no such thing. Now we are in a position to consider another important idea.

Does God Promise Deliverance?

Earlier in this chapter, I explained the difference between the wrath of man and the wrath of God. Nowhere in Scripture does God promise believers deliverance from the wrath of man or tribulation. On the contrary, God repeatedly promises that in this world the church militant will experience plenty of tribulation. What God does promise believers is deliverance from

His wrath, including that divine judgment associated with the Day of the Lord.

This line of thinking leads to the conclusion that the entire period of time between the first and second comings of Jesus will be a time of tribulation, that is, a time in which Christians will experience the wrath of man. Obviously, the church has been going through tribulation from its beginning. I suppose that the only Christians in the history of the world who might have difficulty appreciating this fact are the coddled, protected, largely untested Christians presently living in the United States.

Chinese Christians who were martyred after the communist takeover of their nation in the late 1940s experienced tribulation. Scottish Presbyterians persecuted by the Church of England in the seventeenth century had firsthand knowledge of the wrath of man. English Protestants persecuted at the command of Bloody Queen Mary in the early 1500s knew what tribulation was. And so too did generations of Christians early in the history of the church who suffered horribly at the hands of the Roman empire. I find incredible irony here: When we remember the sufferings and tribulation of millions of believers during the history of the church, there is something bizarre in the spectacle of millions of American Christians who have suffered very little for their faith expecting that they, of all people, would be spared from suffering during some future tribulation!

Hope for the Church Militant

There is another irony in all this. If the pre-tribulationist view of the book of Revelation were correct, this magnificent book would be largely irrelevant to the persecution and suffering of earlier generations of believers. As pre-tribulationists see things, the exhilarating picture of redeemed believers who remained steadfast during persecution and suffering for Christ in Revelation 7 describes not Christians, but the special and separate group of "tribulation saints." But under an amillennial scenario, where tribulation (the wrath of man) is the lot of most Christians during the history of the church, Revelation suddenly becomes the most relevant book in the Bible. Let Satan do to us what he will, the book proclaims, God is still on His throne working out His purposes in the world. No matter how hopeless things may appear, God's triumph is assured. Have hope and do not despair, the last book of the Bible urges believers who are suffering for their faith!

On this view of things, the message of the book of Revelation turns out to be identical with Paul's words in Romans 8:35-39:

> Who shall separate us from the love of Christ? Shall trouble ["tribulation," KJV] or hardship or persecution or famine or nakedness or danger or sword? . . . No, in all these things we are more than conquerors through him who loved us. For I am convinced that neither death nor life, neither angels nor demons, neither the present nor the future, nor any powers, neither height nor depth, nor anything else in all creation, will be able to separate us from the love of God that is in Christ Jesus our Lord.

The book of Revelation is a message of hope to the church militant during its time of tribulation and trouble between the first and second comings of Christ. The church may suffer the wrath of man (tribulation) but it will be delivered from the wrath of God (the Day of the Lord).[5]

QUESTION FOUR: WHAT IF THERE IS NO BIBLICAL DISTINCTION BETWEEN THE RAPTURE AND THE SECOND COMING OF CHRIST?

Pre-tribulationists insist that verses like 1 Thessalonians 4:13-18 and Revelation 19:11-16 refer to two totally different events.

The first is supposed to describe the sudden, secret, any-moment rapture in which Jesus Christ returns in the air for His church. This rapture supposedly will occur *before* the start of the tribulation. Revelation 19:11-16, on the other hand, is explained as an account of the Second Coming in which Christ returns to earth with His church. The Second Coming will occur at the end of the tribulation period. Is there any real basis for this distinction?

For one thing, amillennialists believe that the supposed difference between the visible and public Second Coming and what is described as a *secret* rapture is difficult to justify biblically. When one reads 1 Thessalonians 4:13-18 it is hard to find anything very quiet going on. The passage refers to an archangel *shouting* and a trumpet *blowing*. The event sounds rather public.

More serious is the argument that the rapture and the Second Coming differ in another way. In the rapture, presumably, Christ comes *for* His church; in the Second Coming, He comes *with* His church. How, the premillennialist asks, can Christ come *for* His church and *with* His church at the same time, in the same event? Does this point not oblige us to recognize a difference between the rapture and the Second Coming? Good question, but I don't think it does.

The apparent problem is eliminated by the distinction between the church militant (the church on earth) and the church triumphant (the church in heaven). Once this is remembered, it becomes simple to see how in the same event (the Second Coming) Christ comes *with* the church triumphant and comes *for* the church militant. First Thessalonians 4:13-19 can easily refer to precisely the same event as Revelation 19:11-16.[6]

But of course, the most serious objection to any teaching about a rapture as distinct from the Second Coming has already been presented. If there is no future seven-year tribulation period, then there is no theological reason to distinguish the rapture and the Second Coming as two separate events. There is no reason for any pre-tribulation rapture since there is no *future* tribulation to be rescued from.

QUESTION FIVE: WHAT IF THERE IS NO ESSENTIAL DIFFERENCE BETWEEN OLD TESTAMENT AND NEW TESTAMENT BELIEVERS?

Even though this point is not mentioned earlier in this chapter, it touches on an important issue when comparing amillennial to premillennial pre-tribulation thinking. Almost all pre-tribulationists divide believers of all eras into different groups. For example, the Old Testament saints are made forever distinct from the New Testament church. And this view says, since the church will have been physically removed from the world before the start of the tribulation, the many people who become believers during the tribulation must belong to still a third company. They cannot be part of the church since the composition of the church was completed at the time of the rapture.

Whenever this kind of thinking takes hold, people sometimes tend to think that these different groups end up getting saved through different means. If the major characteristic of salvation for the church is divine grace, some have taught, then perhaps the Old Testament and tribulation saints are saved by some means other than divine grace. I once studied under a pre-tribulationist who taught his students that the Old Testament saints were saved by their obedience to the Mosaic law and that the tribulation saints will be saved by remaining steadfast to the end. This is muddled thinking at best. And, fortunately, most responsible modern pre-tribulationists don't teach this.

Scripture does *not* divide the redeemed of God into two or more different groups who follow two or more different routes to salvation. Romans 4 makes it clear that Abraham was justified by faith just as Christians must be. Abraham's faith was grounded on an atonement that was still future for him. In our case, we look back in time to an atonement completed in the past.

The New Testament repeatedly offers evidence of the continuity between Old Testament and New Testament saints. Paul describes the church as "the Israel of God" (Galatians 6:16), "the circumcision" (Philippians 3:3), and the "seed of Abraham" (Galatians 3:7,29). Peter refers to Christians as "a royal priesthood" and a "peculiar people" (1 Peter 2:9-10). The writer of Hebrews speaks of the church in such Old Testament terms as "Mount Zion" and "the heavenly Jerusalem" (12:22). And so, amillennialists hold that there is only one church, one family of God comprised of all believers from all the ages, all of whom are redeemed in but one way, by grace through faith.

"How is any of this relevant?" some will ask. This is a fair question. It is important to note that some pre-tribulationists, most of them professors in seminaries and Bible colleges, now acknowledge the essential unity of the people of God. But during the years right after my conversion, my teachers drew all kinds of distinctions between Old Testament saints, New Testament saints, tribulation saints, and the like. Some professors taught that members of these different groups were saved in different ways. Claims like these were part of their argument for a pre-tribulation rapture. The rapture, they claimed, ends the church age. If that is so, then the membership of the church would be complete at the time of the rapture. They taught that anyone saved during the tribulation period, then, *must* belong to some group in heaven distinct from the church.

Some of my pre-tribulationist friends today counsel me that my professors forty years ago were out of touch. While it is comforting to hear pre-tribulationist scholars today reject that old distinction between believing Old Testament Jews and the church, the fact remains that much of the pre-tribulationism that pervades the popular, less-sophisticated thought world of televangelists and many preachers still includes the conviction that God has different companies of believers in His kingdom. Wholly apart from disagreements over the details of Bible prophecy, the amillennialist emphasis upon the essential unity of the people of God is a recovery of an important biblical truth. The fact that some pre-tribulationist scholars now share this conviction is a promising sign and may well open up possibilities of greater agreement between them and amillennialists.[7]

QUESTION SIX: WHAT ABOUT THE ANTICHRIST?

In one sense, an answer to this question is not required to support the case against pre-tribulationism. But the doctrine of the Antichrist is so important to many Christians that it might help them to know how the amillennial approach I've been recommending handles this issue.

The first step in understanding how amillennialists handle this issue is that they recognize the distinction between the spirit of Antichrist and specific individuals who function in the role of Antichrist in different places and times. John hints at this distinction in 1 John 2:18 when he not only warns Christians that the Antichrist is coming (future), but also reminds us that many antichrists have already come (past).

Revelation 13 suggests that this spirit of Antichrist assumes both a political and a religious form. The first beast in Revelation 13 symbolizes anti-Christian government that at different times and in different places subjects believers to the wrath of man (tribulation). The second beast symbolizes anti-Christian religion that deceives humans into following some substitute for Christ.

For Christians living in Rome shortly after AD 60, Nero was antichrist. For Chinese Christians who became targets of persecution after the communist takeover in the late 1940s, Mao Tse-Tung was antichrist. It is possible to identify scores of enemies of Christianity during the history of the church who embodied the spirit of Antichrist in different ages and nations.

Hence, amillennialists believe that the pre-tribulationists have wasted time worrying about which world ruler in their time was *the* Antichrist, that is, the one and only Antichrist who would wreak so much havoc during the supposed seven-year tribulation. The spirit of Antichrist has been incarnated in many specific individuals throughout the past and undoubtedly this will continue to be the case in the future.

CONCLUSION

My concern in this chapter has been to challenge pre-tribulationists to think more profoundly about a set of beliefs that too many people know only well enough to parrot what they have heard or read. When I did this myself, years ago when I held similar views, I was shocked to discover the extent to which I was reading a system of belief into the Bible, rather than inferring it from Scripture. My own efforts to dig more deeply into Scripture in this regard had a significant effect on my Christian life. I stopped taking my views on these subjects from others and began to search the Bible for myself.

Now that this chapter is over, let me review what I've done. I've directed your attention to one of ten debates we're examining in this book. I'm confident that many Christians are interested in this debate. In this chapter I've suggested an answer that is not especially popular right now. But popularity, I have argued, can never be a test for truth. I have encouraged you to adopt an independent attitude, to begin thinking about the end times for yourself. But what if you've followed my advice, thought through this issue and find that you disagree with the position taken in this chapter? I think that is still great! The most important thing any teacher can do is get people to think for themselves.[8]

EPILOGUE

❖

Several years ago, I spoke at the International School of Theology at what was then the headquarters of the Campus Crusade organization in Arrowhead Springs, California, just north of San Bernardino. While staying at the hotel on the grounds, I decided to visit the famous underground hot springs that gave the area its name. In order to reach the hot springs, it was necessary to walk down a number of steps leading to where the springs came up in the cavern. It was quite a sight standing in that underground cavern, about fifty feet below the earth's surface.

Bubbling out of numerous cracks in the floor and wall of the underground room was water that had been heated to a high temperature during its journey deep in the earth. I asked my guide why all that hot water came bubbling from the depths at precisely that spot. The guide explained that the cracks in the earth through which the water flowed had been caused by movement in the San Andreas Fault.

Naive as I was, I then asked where the famous fault happened to be. Looking down at his feet and pointing, the guide laughingly informed me that we were standing right on top of the fault line that would someday produce the big earthquake that all of Southern California feared. The next thing I recall is moving faster than I had ever moved in my entire life.

Once I was back on the surface, on top of the underground cavern and its hot springs, I observed how peaceful and serene everything looked, while just below, gigantic forces were at work that someday may bring massive destruction to the area.

To the casual, uninformed observer, contemporary evangelicalism may appear as quiet and peaceful as the pleasant grounds I've just described. But below the surface, there is significant movement and change occurring that could, at any moment, dramatically alter the face of American evangelicalism. Any of the issues we've considered in this book has the potential to produce this kind of upheaval.

This fact helps to explain why it is so important for us to be informed about these issues—and others. But it's also important to notice something else that's been percolating just below the surface of these discussions. I'm referring to the frequent Christian inattention to such things as theology, philosophy, economics, psychology, social theory, and the like. I have no intention of disparaging the richness of Christian *experience* nor of the important role that emotion plays in the Christian life. But Christians who are paying attention only to how they *feel* about religious matters aren't much use to the faith these days.

Confusion about the issues discussed in this book persists because many Christians are not thinking very deeply about important things. The people who operate religious bookstores know how easy it is to sell a book that will make people feel better about this or that. But trying to sell a book that will help Christians *think* more responsibly about some issue or other is a different matter entirely.

Human disagreements are sometimes divided into two types. First, there are what some have termed *disagreements in belief*. Disagreements of this kind typically occur when people differ over some matter of fact. Some examples of this kind of disagreement encountered in this book include: Does the Bible teach that women are not to exercise leadership roles within the church? Does Christianity necessarily discriminate against women in certain respects? Does the Bible condemn divorce under all circumstances? Do liberal social policies injure the poor? Is psychological counseling always in conflict with biblical principles? Do political conservatives really lack proper Christian compassion? These are just a few examples we have covered in this book.

In principle, it would seem that resolving a factual disagreement should be a relatively simple matter. But as we've seen in the case of the issues examined in this book, that is seldom the case. A major factor contributing to this situation is the occasional difficulty we encounter in interpreting some passages of Scripture. Of course, it is also possible that our approach to the Bible may be affected by factors relevant to the second type of human disagreement, those in *attitude*.

A disagreement in belief occurs when one person says, for example, the world is flat while another says the world is round. Once the truth is known, the disagreement should vanish. Of course, the reason the disagreement ceases is because we then know that one person is right and the other is wrong.

A disagreement in attitude occurs when one person says, for example, he approves of political liberalism while another says she disapproves. To some extent, I'm sure, disagreements in attitude may be functions of more basic disagreements in belief. The person who likes liberalism may believe that liberalism, generally speaking, helps people in some way, while the person who disapproves believes that liberalism more often than not is destructive of important personal and social values.

Complicating things even more are situations where Christians bring extra-biblical beliefs and their attitudes and prejudices to their study of the Bible. Whenever this happens, it is hardly surprising when exercises in exegesis (pulling the meaning of Scripture out from the Bible) end up being explorations in eisegesis (reading some meaning into the Bible). Putting one's own ideas into the Word of the Sovereign Lord is serious business. This book has uncovered several situations where this appears to be the case.

Let me close this book by offering a few suggestions to prospective peacemakers on the issues covered in the previous chapters. First, familiarize yourself with the material presented in this book. Is it possible to identify issues of fact that are in disagreement? Then dig deeper to see if you can discover where one set of claims is falsified. For example, in my discussion of reconstructionism, I noted that some opponents of theonomy have described the movement as critical of democracy. We found good reason to dismiss this charge as untrue. Does that piece of information make progress on resolving the dispute over theonomy more likely?

Second, we must pay more attention to how conflicting attitudes affect the disagreement. If people don't like broccoli, I don't know how you can alter their attitude. If people don't like reconstructionists, it's possible that helping them get their information straight may modify the attitude. Or, as in the case of the discussion in this book, it may help them discover new reasons for rejecting theonomy.

Third, practice the assorted advice the apostle Paul gives Christians with regard to disagreements over matters not essential to the integrity of the Christian faith (see Romans 14 and 1 Corinthians 13). Disagreeing is not the worst thing that can happen in our human relationships.

However, neither is turning one's back on the truth simply to avoid unpleasantness a virtue. No religion in the world is more concerned with issues of truth than Christianity. To pretend the truth doesn't exist in some instance or to neglect the defense of the truth in matters central to the Christian faith is a mark of unfaithfulness.

Having said all this, I hope to rejoice over the years at reports that this book has been helpful in some church or community in bridging one great divide or another.

NOTES

❖

Introduction

1. For a more complete account of the important subject of worldview, see Ronald Nash *Worldviews in Conflict* (Grand Rapids, MI: Zondervan, 1992).
2. George Barna, *The Frog in the Kettle* (Ventura, CA: Regal Books, 1990), pages 124-125.
3. Of course, the Christian faith is more than this. In the Bible, God has given us important information in the form of revealed truth. See Ronald Nash, *The Word of God and the Mind of Man* (Phillipsburg, NJ: Presbyterian and Reformed, 1992).
4. Barna, page 125.

Chapter One—The Controversy Over the Pro-Life Movement

1. Paul D. Simmons, a professor of social ethics at Southern Baptist Seminary in Louisville, Kentucky, has published his pro-abortion views in a tract titled *A Theological Response to Fundamentalism on the Abortion Issue* (Washington, DC: Religious Coalition for Abortion Rights Educational Fund, 1985). One would think a professor at a Southern Baptist seminary would fall on the side of life. Another writer claiming evangelical ties is Virginia Ramey Mollenkott whose pro-abortion views are carefully and extensively laid out in an article in an evangelical publication published by the Coalition of Christian Colleges. See Mollenkott, "Reproductive Choice: Basic to Justice for Women," *Christian Scholars Review* 17 (1987–1988), pages 286-293.
2. See Ronald J. Sider, *Completely Pro-Life* (Downers Grove, IL: Inter-Varsity, 1987).
3. The Barna Research Group, Ltd., *Born Again: A Look at Christians in America* (Glendale, CA: The Barna Research Group, Ltd., 1989), pages 53-54. Used by permission.

4. Francis Schaeffer and C. Everett Koop, *Whatever Happened to the Human Race?* in *The Complete Works of Francis A. Schaeffer,* vol. 5 (Westchester, IL: Crossway, 1985), page 281.
5. Schaeffer and Koop, pages 283-284.
6. Charles Colson, "Seamless Garment or Straightjacket?" *Christianity Today*, November 4, 1988, page 72.
7. See Robert D. Orr, M.D., David L. Schiedermayer, M.D., and David B. Biebel, D.Min., *Life and Death Decisions* (Colorado Springs, CO: NavPress, 1991), pages 55-56, 59-60.
8. Orr, Schiedermayer, and Biebel, page 55; see also Daniel Callahan, "How Technology Is Reframing the Abortion Debate," *Hastings Center Report*, February 1986, 16 (1), pages 33-34.
9. Carol McMillan, *Women, Reason, and Nature* (Princeton, NJ: Princeton University Press, 1982), pages 115-116.
10. Shulamith Firestone, *The Dialectic of Sex: The Case for Feminist Revolution* (London: Women's Press, 1979), page 73.
11. James L. Sauer, "The Feminist Mistake," *The New American*, January 15, 1990, page 40.
12. See Mollenkott, pages 286-293. This article received a powerful rebuttal from philosopher George Mavrodes: "Abortion and Imagination: Reflections on Mollenkott's 'Reproductive Choice,'" *Christian Scholars Review* 18 (1988–1989), pages 168-170. Mollenkott's response to Mavrodes (pages 171-172 of the same issue) is notable for having missed Mavrodes' point completely.
13. Mollenkott, page 292.
14. Arthur Brestel, "Response to Mollenkott," *Christian Scholars Review* 18 (1988–1989), page 102.
15. "Abortion Does *Not* Liberate Women" (Kansas City, MO: Feminists for Life, n.d.). Subsequent quotations come from the unnumbered pages of this pamphlet.
16. Ronald J. Sider, *Completely Pro-Life* (Downers Grove, IL: InterVarsity, 1987), page 44.
17. Sider, *Completely Pro-Life*, page 44.
18. Ronald J. Sider, "Abortion Is Not the Only Issue," *Christianity Today*, July 14, 1989, page 28.
19. Richard John Neuhaus, *Religion and Society Report*, October 1988, page 3.
20. Neuhaus, page 5.
21. Neuhaus, page 4.
22. Neuhaus, page 5.
23. Neuhaus, page 4.

24. Neuhaus, page 4.
25. Charles E. White, "Why Abortion Matters Most," *Christianity Today*, July 14, 1989, page 35.
26. White, page 35.
27. White, page 34.
28. White, page 36.
29. For more detail, see Ronald Nash, *Poverty and Wealth* (Dallas, TX: Probe Books/Word Publishing, 1992).
30. Another example that could be discussed at greater length is the JustLife support for liberal welfare programs, which we now know are counterproductive and injurious to the poor. See Nash, *Poverty and Wealth.*
31. Neuhaus, page 4.
32. White, page 36.
33. White, page 36.

Chapter Two—The Controversy Over Women Leaders in the Church

1. See Paul K. Jewett, *Man as Male and Female* (Grand Rapids, MI: Eerdmans, 1975), pages 118, 134, 138.
2. Robert K. Johnston, *Evangelicals at an Impasse* (Atlanta, GA: John Knox, 1979), page 58. Johnston refers his readers to Jewett, pages 112-113.
3. Virginia Mollenkott, "A Conversation with Virginia Mollenkott," *The Other Side*, May-June 1976, page 22.
4. Virginia Mollenkott, "Evangelicalism: A Feminist Perspective," *Union Seminary Quarterly Review* 32 (Winter 1977), pages 95, 97, 99.
5. Donald Bloesch, *The Battle for the Trinity* (Ann Arbor, MI: Servant, 1985), page 5.
6. As we'll see in the next chapter, feminist extremists demonstrate a lot of sympathy for lesbianism. The Evangelical Women's Caucus, perhaps the major organization of evangelical feminists, split in 1986 over the issue of whether a lesbian presence would be recognized within the group.
7. Johnston, page 13.
8. *Christianity Today*, April 9, 1990, pages 36-37. The ad also appeared in other publications as well as in other issues of *Christianity Today*.
9. It appears that some signers were evangelical feminists with a propensity to subordinate Scripture to their extra-biblical test of feminism. Now that I've noted this, the rest of my discussion will

deal with the document as a statement of the positions held by the biblical equalitarians who signed it.

10. For examples of how traditionalists handle such texts, see *Recovering Biblical Manhood and Womanhood*, John Piper and Wayne Grudem, eds. (Wheaton, IL: Crossway, 1991).

11. The case of Galatians 3:28 suggests that traditionalists have their problem texts, as do equalitarians. Later, I'll point out how traditionalists handle this verse.

12. Don Carson, a traditionalist, does an able job in explaining many interpretations of this passage. See "'Silent in the Churches': On the Role of Women in 1 Corinthians 14:33b-36," *Recovering Biblical Manhood and Womanhood*, pages 140-153. Equalitarians complain that his presentation has gaps and that his traditionalist conclusion appears plausible because it depends on traditionalist assumptions.

13. W. Ward Gasque, "Response," *Women, Authority and the Bible*, Alvera Mickelsen, ed. (Downers Grove, IL: InterVarsity, 1986), page 191.

14. Scott E. McClelland, "The New Reality in Christ: Perspectives from Biblical Studies," *Gender Matters*, June Steffensen Hagen, ed. (Grand Rapids, MI: Zondervan, 1990), page 72.

15. This sentence is interesting. It points to a problem in Ephesus similar to that raised by anti-evangelical and anti-Christian feminists in their move toward a goddess religion.

16. McClelland, page 72.

17. McClelland, page 74.

18. Bruce Barron, "Putting Women in their Place: 1 Timothy 2 and Evangelical Views of Women in Church Leadership," *Journal of the Evangelical Theological Society*, 33 (1990), pages 451-459.

19. Barron, page 455.

20. For a lengthy introduction to Gnosticism, see Ronald Nash, *The Gospel and the Greeks* (Dallas, TX: Probe, 1991), part 3. One of Gnosticism's tenets was that the spiritually enlightened, those who had experienced "gnosis," would possess certain secret knowledge unattainable by those outside the Gnostic cult.

21. Barron, page 458.

22. Barron, page 456.

23. Barron, page 456.

24. From the preface to *Recovering Biblical Manhood & Womanhood*, page xiv.

25. It is interesting to see how these cases are handled by various

writers in *Recovering Biblical Manhood & Womanhood*. In most cases, I'm sure, traditionalists would welcome somewhat stronger arguments.

26. S. Lewis Johnson, "Role Distinctions in the Church: Galatians 3:28," *Recovering Biblical Manhood & Womanhood*, pages 154-164.
27. Johnson, page 163.
28. Johnson, page 164.
29. Piper and Grudem, "An Overview of Central Concerns: Questions and Answers," *Recovering Biblical Manhood & Womanhood*, pages 68-69.
30. See Piper and Grudem, pages 79-80.
31. Piper and Grudem, page 70.
32. Piper and Grudem, page 70.
33. See Barron, pages 451-459.
34. Quoted material from Barron, pages 458-459. The names for the four options are mine.

Chapter Three—The Controversy Over Radical Feminism

1. Christina Hoff Sommers, "Feminism and the College Curriculum," *Imprimis*, June 1990, page 2.
2. Sommers, page 2.
3. Sommers, page 4.
4. William Oddie, *What Will Happen to God?* (London: SPCK, 1984), page 6.
5. For a detailed but simple introduction to Gnosticism, see Ronald Nash, *The Gospel and the Greeks* (Dallas, TX: Probe, 1991), part 3.
6. Denise Lardner Carmody, *Feminism and Christianity* (Nashville, TN: Abingdon, 1982), page 27.
7. Pantheism is an approach to religion that blurs the distinction between God and the world. The god of pantheism is not the transcendent Creator of the world since pantheists deny any creation. Rather, they believe the world itself is divine. Pantheism is achieving greater popularity in the West through the New Age movement.
8. Carmody, page 27.
9. Naomi Goldenberg, *Changing of the Gods* (Boston, MA: Beacon, 1979), page 4.
10. Starhawk, *The Spiral Dance: A Rebirth of the Ancient Religion of the Great Goddess* (San Francisco, CA: Harper and Row, 1979), page 9.
11. Elizabeth Achtemeier, foreword to *The Battle for the Trinity* by

Donald G. Bloesch (Ann Arbor, MI: Servant, 1985), page xii.

12. Achtemeier, foreword to *The Battle for the Trinity*, pages xii-xiii.

13. Rosemary Radford Reuther, *Sexism and God-Talk: Toward a Feminist Theology* (Boston, MA: Beacon, 1983), pages 18-19.

14. Rosemary Radford Reuther, "Feminist Interpretation: A Method of Correlation," *Feminist Interpretation of the Bible*, Letty Russell, ed. (Philadelphia, PA: Westminister, 1985), page 117.

15. Reuther, *Sexism and God-Talk*, pages 48-49.

16. Elizabeth Achtemeier, "Female Language for God: Should the Church Adopt It?" *The Hermeneutical Quest*, Donald G. Miller, ed. (Allison Park, PA: Pickwick, 1986), page 107.

17. Elizabeth Schussler Fiorenza, "The Will to Choose or to Reject," *Feminist Interpretation of the Bible*, page 128.

18. Elizabeth Schussler Fiorenza, *Bread Not Stone: The Challenge of Feminist Biblical Interpretation* (Boston, MA: Beacon, 1984), page 14.

19. Achtemeier, foreword to *The Battle for the Trinity*, page xi.

20. Elizabeth Achtemeier, "Renewed Appreciation for an Unchanging Story," *Christian Century*, June 13-20, 1990, page 598.

21. Achtemeier, "Renewed Appreciation," page 598. Quotes immediately following are from the same source.

22. Naomi Janowitz and Maggie Wening, "Sabbath Prayers for Women," *WomanSpirit Rising*, Carol P. Christ and Judith Plaskow, eds. (San Francisco, CA: Harper and Row, 1979), page 176.

23. *WomanSpirit Rising*, page 168.

24. Starhawk, "Witchcraft and Women's Culture," *WomanSpirit Rising*, page 263.

25. See Virginia Mollenkott, *The Divine Feminine: The Biblical Imagery of God as Female* (New York: Crossroad, 1983), pages 89-90.

26. Achtemeier, "Female Language for God," page 100.

27. Achtemeier, page 101.

28. *National and International Religion Report*, vol. 4, no. 18, August 27, 1990, page 4.

29. *National and International Religion Report*, page 4.

30. *National and International Religion Report*, page 4.

31. Achtemeier, "Female Language for God," page 107.

32. Achtemeier, page 108.

33. Achtemeier, pages 108-109.

34. Donald C. Bloesch, *The Battle for the Trinity* (Ann Arbor, MI: Servant, 1985), page 40.

35. Bloesch, page 39.
36. Bloesch, page 39.
37. Oddie, page 22.
38. June Steffensen Hagen, ed., *Gender Matters* (Grand Rapids, MI: Zondervan, 1990. To be fair to the evangelical college with which the contributors were once associated, almost all of them now work for other organizations.
39. Terri Graves Taylor, "Agenda Matters," *Genesis*, April 9, 1990, page 6.

Chapter Four—The Controversy Over Divorce and Remarriage

1. Churches like First Evangelical Free Church of Fullerton, CA (Charles Swindoll, senior pastor; Gary Richmond, pastor of ministry to single parents), and Willowcreek Church in South Barrington, IL (Bill Hybels, senior pastor), among many others across the country, are ministering to these hurting people.
2. Craig Blomberg, "Marriage, Divorce, Remarriage, and Celibacy: An Exegesis of Matthew 19:3-12," *Trinity Journal* 11 (New Series) (1990), page 189.
3. Blomberg, page 189.
4. The best-known book defending the *A* position is by William A. Heth and Gordon J. Wenham, *Jesus and Divorce* (Nashville, TN: Thomas Nelson, 1985).
5. See *Christianity Today*, June 6, 1980, page 27.
6. In a *Christianity Today* poll, 64 percent of polled clergy agreed with the *B* position. The survey did not break down the three versions of the *B* position that I have identified. While the percentages of clergy and the general public were almost the same on option *A*, only 40 percent of the general public identified *B* as their view. Far more people preferred the lenient views (*C* and *D*).
7. One widely read book that defends position B2 is by John Murray, *Divorce* (Philadelphia, PA: Committee on Christian Education, Orthodox Presbyterian Church, 1953). Murray was, for many years, professor of theology at Westminster Theological Seminary in Philadelphia.
8. Samuel J. Mikolaski, "Divorce," *Encyclopedia of Biblical and Christian Ethics*, R. K. Harrison, ed. (Nashville, TN: Thomas Nelson, 1987), page 115.
9. Mikolaski, page 114.
10. D. J. Atkinson, "Divorce," *Evangelical Dictionary of Theology*, Walter A. Elwell, ed. (Grand Rapids, MI: Baker, 1984), page 324

11. Atkinson, page 324.
12. "Ad Interim Committee on Marriage, Divorce, and Remarriage," Minutes of the Nineteenth General Assembly of the Presbyterian Church in America (1991), page 644.
13. Obviously, the Old Testament is written in Hebrew, not Greek. *Porneia* appears in the Septuagint, the Greek translation of the Hebrew Old Testament. The Hebrew equivalent of *porneia* appears in the Hebrew text.
14. Blomberg, page 192.
15. Blomberg, page 192.
16. Blomberg, pages 195-196.
17. Blomberg, page 196.
18. Blomberg, page 196.
19. Report to the 1991 General Assembly of the Presbyterian Church in America, page 653.
20. Blomberg, page 196. His remarks presuppose that the divorces he has in view occurred on biblical grounds.
21. Report on Divorce to the 1991 General Assembly of the Presbyterian Church in America, page 654.

Chapter Five—The Controversy Over Psychology and Counseling
 1. Bernie Zilbergeld, *The Shrinking of America: Myths of Psychological Change* (Boston, MA: Little, Brown, 1983).
 2. Paul C. Vitz, *Psychology as Religion: The Cult of Self Worship* (Grand Rapids, MI: Eerdmans, 1977); William Kirk Kilpatrick, *Psychological Seduction: The Failure of Modern Psychology* (Nashville, TN: Thomas Nelson, 1983); Mark P. Cosgrove, *Psychology Gone Awry: An Analysis of Psychological World Views* (Grand Rapids, MI: Zondervan, 1979); Martin and Diedre Bobgan, *The Psychological Way/The Spiritual Way* (Minneapolis, MN: Bethany, 1979).
 3. Martin and Diedre Bobgan, *Psycho-Heresy 1* (Santa Barbara, CA: EastGate Publishers, 1987).
 4. Vitz.
 5. Vitz, page 67.
 6. Larry Crabb, *Basic Principles of Biblical Counseling* (Grand Rapids, MI: Zondervan, 1975), page 41.
 7. See Frank Minirth and Walter Byrd, *Christian Psychiatry*, rev. ed. (Old Tappan, New Jersey: Fleming H. Revell Co., 1991); also Gary Collins, *Effective Counseling* (Carol Stream, IL: Creation House, 1972); Gary Collins, *Can You Trust Psychology?* (Downers Grove, IL: Inter-Varsity, 1988); Larry Crabb, *Basic Principles of Biblical Counseling*

(Grand Rapids, MI: Zondervan, 1975); Larry Crabb, *Effective Biblical Counseling* (Grand Rapids, MI: Zondervan, 1977); and Larry Crabb, *Inside Out* (Colorado Springs, CO: NavPress, 1988).

8. See Dave Hunt and T. A. McMahon, *The Seduction of Christianity* (Eugene, OR: Harvest, 1985), page 131; also Kilpatrick, page 30.

9. Mark McMinn and James Foster, *Christians in the Crossfire: Guarding Your Mind Against Manipulation and Self-Deception* (Newberg, Oregon: The Barclay Press, 1990), page 103.

10. Crabb, *Inside Out*, page 13.

11. Collins points out that in the few studies that have been done on the success of religious counselors, we just do not have enough information to predict the percentage of success of these counselors. Collins, *Can You Trust Psychology?*, pages 60-64.

12. Collins, page 102.

13. Zilbergeld.

14. Martin and Deidre Bobgan, *The Psychological Way/The Spiritual Way*, quoted in Collins, *Can You Trust Psychology?*, page 114.

15. Collins, page 115.

16. See Collins, pages 44-48; and Crabb, *Effective Biblical Counseling*. Crabb's entire book is dedicated to encouraging lay counselors and helping professionals maintain biblical integrity in their counseling.

17. Collins, *Can You Trust Psychology?*, pages 46-47.

Chapter Six—The Controversy Over the Health and Wealth Gospel

1. D. R. McConnell, *A Different Gospel* (Peabody, MA: Hendrickson, 1988), page xvi.

2. McConnell, page xvi.

3. Jack Kelley, "TV Minister's Star on the Rise," *USA Today*, October 19, 1990, page 6A.

4. *USA Today*, page 6A.

5. Quoted in *USA Today*, page 6A.

6. *Prime Time Live*, November 21, 1991. Tape on file.

7. *Prime Time Live*, November 21, 1991.

8. Benny Hinn, *Good Morning, Holy Spirit* (Nashville, TN: Thomas Nelson, 1990).

9. See "Benny Hinn: Best-Selling Author Admits Mistakes, Vows Changes," *Christianity Today*, October 28, 1991, pages 44-46.

10. See "Benny Hinn," page 44.

11. Charles Farah, *This Cancer Kills: A Critical Analysis of the Roots and Fruits of "Faith-Formula" Theology* (Portland, OR: Charis Life, 1982), page 15.

12. McConnell, page xvii.
13. Kenneth Hagin, "Healing: The Father's Provision," *Word of Faith*, August 1977, page 9.
14. McConnell, page 155.
15. McConnell, page 155.
16. See McConnell, pages 80ff. See also Dennis Hollinger, "Enjoying God Forever: An Historical/Sociological Profile of the Health and Wealth Gospel," *Trinity Journal* 9 (1988), page 133.
17. Don Carson, *Showing the Spirit* (Grand Rapids, MI: Baker, 1987), page 175.
18. James Packer, *Keep in Step With the Spirit* (Old Tappan, NJ: Revell, 1984), page 194.
19. Packer, page 195.
20. McConnell, page 158.
21. McConnell, page 159.
22. McConnell, page 159.
23. Kenneth Copeland, *The Laws of Prosperity* (Fort Worth, TX: Copeland Publications, 1974), pages 18-20.
24. As cited by Bruce Barron, *The Health and Wealth Gospel* (Downers Grove, IL: InterVarsity, 1987), page 89. See Gloria Copeland, *God's Will Is Prosperity* (Tulsa, OK: Harrison, 1978), pages 48-52.
25. McConnell, page 176.
26. From Tilton's TV program *Success 'N Life*, recorded December 2, 1990; quotes provided with permission by the Christian Research Institute (CRI), P.O. Box 500, San Juan Capistrano, CA 92693-0500.
27. From *Success 'N Life*, recorded December 27, 1990; quote provided by CRI.
28. James R. Goff, Jr., "The Faith that Claims," *Christianity Today*, February 19, 1990, page 18.
29. William W. Menzies, "Will Charismatics Go Cultic?" *Christianity Today*, March 3, 1989, page 59 (emphasis added).
30. Menzies, page 59.
31. Goff, page 18.
32. McConnell, page 187.
33. Harold Lindsell, in foreword to *The Agony of Deceit*, Michael Horton, ed. (Chicago, IL: Moody, 1990), no pagination.
34. See McConnell.
35. Menzies, page 59.
36. Menzies, page 59.
37. Horton, page 104.

38. Menzies, page 59.
39. See "Benny Hinn," pages 44-46.
40. From "Benny Hinn," pages 44-46.
41. Randy Frame, "Same Old Benny Hinn, Critics Say," *Christianity Today*, October 5, 1992, page 53.
42. Rod Rosenbladt, "Who Do TV Preachers Say that I Am?" *The Agony of Deceit*, page 116, 118-119.
43. Kenneth Copeland, *Word of Faith* (Forth Worth, TX: Copeland Ministries, 1980), page 14.
44. Kenneth E. Hagin, *Zoe: The God-Kind of Life* (Tulsa, OK: Faith Library, 1981), page 40.
45. Paul Crouch, "Praise the Lord," Trinity Broadcasting Network, July 7, 1986.
46. Horton, page 124.
47. Kenneth Copeland, *Now Are We in Christ Jesus* (Fort Worth, TX: Copeland Publications, n.d.), page 24.

Chapter Seven—The Controversy Over Christian Involvement in Politics

1. For examples of public policies that have done precisely this, see Ronald Nash, *Social Justice and the Christian Church* (Lanham, MD: University Press of America, 1991).
2. In this introductory discussion, there is no need to explore how such factors as rape or threats to the life of the mother may complicate the ethical issues in the thinking of some.
3. By "double-taxation," I am referring to parents being required to support the public schools regardless of the education children receive there and also bearing the added expense of tuition costs if they choose to send their children to private schools. For more on school choice, see Ronald Nash, *The Closing of the American Heart: What's Really Wrong with America's Schools* (Dallas, TX: Probe, 1990).
4. For my own efforts along these lines, see Ronald Nash, *Poverty and Wealth* (Dallas, TX: Probe, 1992); *Freedom, Justice and the State* (Lanham, MD: University Press of America, 1980); and *Social Justice and the Christian Church*. The bibliographies in these books serve to direct the interested reader to other literature.
5. For a defense of this claim, see Ronald Nash, "What do the Evangelicals Want?" *Religious Resurgence and Politics in the Contemporary World*, Emile Sahliyeh, ed. (Albany, NY: State University of New York Press, 1987); also *Piety and Politics,* Richard John

Neuhaus and Michael Cromartie, eds. (Washington, DC: Ethics and Public Policy Center, 1987).

6. The cause of family choice in education is also supported by many Christians who are moderate liberals. For a discussion of the family choice issue, see Nash, *The Closing of the American Heart*.

7. I provide detail about this evangelical mainstream in chapter 2 of *Evangelicals in America* (Nashville, TN: Abingdon Press, 1987).

8. For an example of what I believe is a better approach to economics and the defense of capitalism, see Nash, *Poverty and Wealth*.

9. See Nash, chapter 11, *Poverty and Wealth*.

10. See Nash, chapters 12–13, *Poverty and Wealth*.

11. Here is a short list of such books: Robert G. Clouse, *The Cross and the Flag* (Carol Stream, IL: Creation House, 1972); Richard V. Pierard, *The Unequal Yoke* (Philadelphia, PA: J. B. Lippincott, 1970); Vernon Grounds, *Evangelicalism and Social Responsibility* (Scottsdale, PA: Herald Press, 1969).

12. See Humberto Belli and Ronald Nash, *Beyond Liberation Theology* (Grand Rapids, MI: Baker, 1992).

13. Some economists have criticized the depth of Sider's understanding of capitalism, which, they say, allows for so much governmental intervention that it comes across more like a diluted socialism than a robust market system. In my book *Poverty and Wealth* (see chapter 11), I insist on treating an interventionist economic system like Sider's as something quite different from capitalism.

14. The movement's opposition to Strategic Defense Initiative (SDI) is strange, given its opposition to any use of nuclear weapons as a deterrent. SDI is a strategy of protecting our nation from other countries' nuclear weapons by non-nuclear means.

15. Bernard Adeney, "Is Nuclear Deterrence Acceptable?" *Transformation*, January/March 1988, page 1.

16. Adeney, page 1.

17. Dean C. Curry, "Response to Bernard Adeney," *Transformation*, January/March 1988, page 16.

18. Richard John Neuhaus, "Repression Envy and 'Biblical Politics,'" *The Religion and Society Report*, March 1988, page 6. It is impossible to say everything in one short chapter. For additional material on the Sojourners movement's alliance with the far left, see Humberto Belli and Ronald Nash, *Beyond Liberation Theology* (Grand Rapids, MI: Baker, 1992), pages 76-79. This book also describes the troubling fascination with Marxism found among some self-described evangelicals.

19. Clark Pinnock, "A Pilgrimage in Political Theology," *Liberation Theology*, Ronald Nash, ed. (Grand Rapids, MI: Baker, 1988), page 106.
20. Pinnock, page 106.
21. Pinnock, page 111.
22. Pinnock, page 112.
23. Pinnock, page 112.
24. Pinnock, page 114.
25. Dean C. Curry and Myron S. Augsburger, "The Perils of Contemporary Pacifism," *Nuclear Arms: Two Views on World Peace* (Waco, TX: Word Books, 1987), page 121. Jim Wallis affirms moral equivalence in *Agenda for a Biblical People* (San Francisco, CA: Harper and Row, 1984), pages 56-72.
26. Many people appeal to the notion of justice; it is much more difficult to find someone who can explain what justice is. See Nash, chapter 2, *Freedom, Justice and the State*; and Nash, chapters 3–6, *Social Justice and the Christian Church*.
27. For one example, see Charles Murray, *Losing Ground: American Social Policy 1950–1980* (New York: Basic Books, 1984). Also helpful are the many publications by black economists Walter Williams and Thomas Sowell. Much of this is summarized in Nash, *Poverty and Wealth*.
28. Dean C. Curry, *World Without Tyranny* (Westchester, IL: Crossway Books, 1989), page 103.
29. Curry, page 104.
30. As examples, see Nash, *Social Justice and the Christian Church* and *Freedom, Justice and the State*.
31. Curry, *World Without Tyranny*, page 100.
32. Curry, page 102.

Chapter Eight—The Controversy Over Christian Reconstructionists

1. The civil code of the Pentateuch would include the large body of law outside of the Ten Commandments.
2. Note that all pre-tribulationists are premillennialists.
3. For an interesting, amillennial interpretation of the book of Revelation, see William Hendriksen, *More Than Conquerors* (Grand Rapids, MI: Baker, 1940).
4. For any curious readers, I am not a postmillennialist. It follows, therefore, that I am also not a theonomist.
5. Obviously, any Christian could come to believe that he should seek

to have an impact on unbiblical features of society without also being a postmillennialist.

6. One example of an evangelical scholar who is both a reconstructionist and a postmillennialist without also being a theonomist is Dr. John Jefferson Davis, professor of theology at Gordon-Conwell Theological Seminary and the author of a number of important books on Christian theology and ethics.

7. Gary DeMar, *The Debate Over Christian Reconstructionism* (Atlanta, GA: American Vision, 1988), page 59. At the time he wrote the book, DeMar used the term "Christian reconstructionists." In private conversation, however, DeMar acknowledges the distinction I've made between reconstructionists and theonomists and notes that this passage was intended to describe theonomists.

8. Greg L. Bahnsen and Kenneth L. Gentry, Jr., *House Divided* (Tyler, TX: Institute for Christian Economics, 1989), pages 140-141.

9. Bahnsen and Gentry, page 141.

10. Greg Bahnsen, *Theonomy in Christian Ethics* (Nutley, NJ: Craig Press, 1979).

11. Dave Hunt, *Whatever Happened to Heaven?* (Eugene, OR: Harvest, 1988), page 43.

12. Hunt, page 76.

13. Anyone who has read Hunt's book *Whatever Happened to Heaven?* knows that he has little to say about heaven in that book. For Hunt, the word *heaven* is simply a euphemism for the rapture. What really angers Hunt is not that the theonomists are ignoring heaven, but that they are ignoring one of Hunt's pet doctrines, the pre-tribulation rapture. Since theonomists are postmillennialists, it follows that they reject pre-tribulationism and its view of the rapture. But surely a Christian can disagree with the doctrine of the rapture without rejecting the importance of heaven. Has Dave Hunt really played fair in his attack on theonomy?

14. Clearly, this view that Christians should abandon culture is not held by most premillennialists, or even all dispensationalists.

15. Hal Lindsey, *The Road to Holocaust* (New York: Bantam Books, 1989), page 3.

16. Lindsey, pages 29-30.

17. See Rodney Clapp, "Democracy Is Heresy," *Christianity Today*, February 20, 1987, page 17.

18. Gary DeMar, "A Theonomic Response to 'Civic Responsibility in a Democratic, Pluralistic Republic,'" Unpublished paper (Atlanta, GA: American Vision, n.d.), page 3.

19. Greg Bahnsen, "The Theonomic Position," *God and Politics*, Gary Scott Smith, ed. (Phillipsburg, NJ: Presbyterian and Reformed, 1989), page 53.

20. Gary DeMar, *The Debate Over Christian Reconstructionism* (Atlanta, GA: American Vision, 1988), page 63.

21. Bahnsen and Gentry, page 70.

22. Bahnsen and Gentry, page 71.

23. Bahnsen, "The Theonomic Position," page 24.

24. See Charles Ryrie, "The End of the Law," *Bibliotheca Sacra*, vol. 124 (1967), pages 239-242.

25. Bahnsen, "The Theonomic Position," page 24. The theonomist principles justify the repudiation of the ceremonial laws of the Old Testament, that is, those dealing with animal sacrifices. They are repealed in the New Testament.

26. The theonomist position is superior in at least one instance. The sin of bestiality is not mentioned in the New Testament. But no Christian I know regards such acts as a sexual option for believers. And so here is one example of an Old Testament law not repeated in the New Testament that continues to apply.

27. The statement that "the Christian is obligated to keep the whole law of God as a pattern of sanctification" should not pass unnoticed. Bahnsen does not promote the whole law of God as a pattern of *justification*. We can be justified only by faith. But he maintains that God's law functions as a pattern of sanctification, even though the power for sanctification must come from God (Galatians 2:20). Greg Bahnsen, *Theonomy in Christian Ethics* (Nutley, NJ: Craig Press, 1977), page xiii.

28. Bahnsen, "The Theonomic Position," page 24.

29. Bahnsen, "The Theonomic Position," page 32.

30. Bahnsen, "The Theonomic Position," page 33.

31. John M. Frame, "The One, The Many, and Theonomy," *Theonomy, A Reformed Critique*, William S. Barker and W. Robert Godfrey, eds. (Grand Rapids, MI: Zondervan, 1990), page 93.

32. Some of the worst public relations problems theonomists have result from their frequent talk about public executions by stoning. Since theonomists themselves admit that even if we grant the validity of the interpretive process that is supposed to support this view, the process itself won't be possible until all the pieces for a theonomist society are in place, something that won't be the case for possibly hundreds of years. Bahnsen has urged theonomists to drop all this useless talk about specific punishments and allow future generations

to worry about the matter. See Bahnsen, "The Theonomic Position,"
page 268.

Chapter Nine—The Controversy Over Lordship Salvation

1. John F. MacArthur, Jr., *The Gospel According to Jesus* (Grand Rapids, MI: Zondervan, 1988).
2. John F. MacArthur, Jr., "Faith According to the Apostle James," *Journal of the Evangelical Theological Society*, vol. 33 (1990), page 13.
3. Zane Hodges, *The Gospel Under Siege* (Dallas, TX: Redencion Viva, 1981).
4. Zane Hodges, *Absolutely Free* (Grand Rapids, MI: Zondervan, 1989).
5. Charles C. Ryrie, *So Great Salvation* (Wheaton, IL: Victor, 1989).
6. Livingston Blauvelt, Jr., "Does the Bible Teach Lordship Salvation?" *Bibliotheca Sacra*, January-March 1986, page 37.
7. Arthur W. Pink, *Studies on Saving Faith* (Swengal, PA: Reiner Publications, n.d.), pages 12-13.
8. John R. W. Stott, *Basic Christianity* (Grand Rapids, MI: Eerdmans, 1958), page 114.
9. MacArthur, *The Gospel According to Jesus*, page xiii.
10. Charles C. Ryrie, *Balancing the Christian Life* (Chicago, IL: Moody, 1969), page 170.
11. MacArthur is referring here to Lewis Sperry Chafer's *Systematic Theology*, vol. 3, page 385.
12. MacArthur, *The Gospel According to Jesus*, page 16.
13. MacArthur, page 17.
14. MacArthur, page 23.
15. Hodges, *The Gospel Under Siege*, page 14.
16. Kenneth L. Gentry, "The Great Option: A Study of the Lordship Controversy," *Baptist Reformation Review*, vol. 5 (Spring 1976), page 50.
17. Ryrie, *Balancing the Christian Life*, page 21.
18. Hodges, *Absolutely Free*, page 213.
19. Hodges, page 216.
20. Hodges, page 216.
21. Hodges, page 220.
22. MacArthur, *The Gospel According to Jesus*, page 33.
23. MacArthur, "Faith According to the Apostle James," pages 14-16.
24. MacArthur, page 16.
25. MacArthur, pages 16-17.
26. MacArthur, pages 20-21.

27. Hodges, *Absolutely Free*, page 18.
28. Hodges, page 19.
29. Hodges, page 98.
30. Hodges, page 160.
31. Hodges, pages 145-146.
32. Hodges, page 146.
33. Walter Bauer, *A Greek-English Lexicon of the New Testament and Other Early Christian Literature*, William F. Arndt and F. Wilbur Gingrich, trans. (Chicago, IL: University of Chicago Press, 1952, 1957), pages 517-518.
34. L. S. Chafer, *Systematic Theology (Vol. 3): Soteriology* (Dallas, TX: Dallas Theological Seminary Press, 1948), page 373.
35. Gentry, page 60.
36. James I. Packer, *Evangelism and the Sovereignty of God* (Downers Grove, IL: InterVarsity, 1961), pages 72-73.
37. MacArthur, *The Gospel According to Jesus*, page 32.
38. MacArthur, page 163.
39. Ryrie, *So Great Salvation*, page 73.
40. Ryrie, page 73.
41. See Ryrie, page 74; also Hodges, *Absolutely Free*, pages 170-172.
42. Gentry, page 66.
43. Gentry, page 68.
44. Gentry, page 69.
45. S. Lewis Johnson, Jr., "How Faith Works," *Christianity Today*, September 22, 1989, page 25.
46. Charles C. Ryrie, ed., *The Ryrie Study Bible* (Chicago, IL: Moody, 1978), pages 1859-1860.

Chapter Ten—The Controversy Over the End Times

1. I have used the footnote notation in the *New International Version* for an alternate reading of the last word of the verse.
2. Again, I have used a perfectly acceptable alternate reading of the Hebrew original from the NIV footnote reference.
3. Once again, I have used the alternate reading of the Hebrew original from the NIV footnote reference.
4. Nothing in verse 27 requires us to believe that the covenant will last only seven years. What is in view in the last seven years is the period of time between the beginning of Jesus' public ministry and the first few years of the church during which the new covenant is first witnessed to by Jesus, then instituted by Him at the Last Supper, and finally proclaimed by the early church.

5. See 2 Peter 3:3-14.

6. When Paul speaks of the dead in Christ rising first, he clearly is not suggesting that dead saints have been waiting in the grave for the Second Coming. He is referring to the resurrection of the bodies of dead saints. Obviously, the members of the church triumphant are with Christ during the time between death and the resurrection. See Luke 23:42-43, Philippians 1:13-23.

7. Some critics of the position defended in this chapter point to several texts that they believe create problems for this view. Romans 10:1, one of these, reads, "Brethren, my heart's desire and prayer to God for Israel is, that they might be saved." All Paul is saying here is that he longs for and prays for the salvation of unbelieving Jews. He prays that they might become part of the one Body of Christ. Another text they point to is 1 Corinthians 10:32, which says, "Give none offence, neither to the Jews, nor to the Gentiles, nor to the church of God." It is difficult to see what the problem here is supposed to be. Paul is simply urging Christians to do or say nothing that will offend fellow Christians or unbelieving Jews or Gentiles.

8. For readers with further interest in the issues covered in this chapter, I can recommend the following books: George E. Ladd, *The Blessed Hope* (Grand Rapids, MI: Eerdmans, 1956); Oswald T. Allis, *Prophecy and the Church* (Grand Rapids, MI: Baker, 1977 reprint); William Hendriksen, *More Than Conquerors* (Grand Rapids, MI: Baker, 1940); Floyd E. Hamilton, *The Basis of Millennial Faith* (Grand Rapids, MI: Eerdmans, 1942); Archibald Hughes, *A New Heaven and a New Earth* (Philadelphia, PA: Presbyterian and Reformed, 1958); Albertus Pieters, *The Seed of Abraham* (Grand Rapids, MI: Eerdmans, 1950); and Loraine Boettner, *The Millennium* (Philadelphia, PA: Presbyterian and Reformed, 1987).